THE BROKEN CHRISTIAN

A HOPE-FILLED JOURNEY
TOWARD REDEMPTION

MARIO M. INGLIMA

THE BROKEN CHRISTIAN

A HOPE-FILLED JOURNEY TOWARD REDEMPTION

Charleston, SC
www.PalmettoPublishing.com

The Broken Christian

Copyright © 2021 by Mario M. Inglima

First Edition

Hardcover ISBN: 978-1-63837-650-7
Paperback ISBN: 978-1-63837-248-6
eBook ISBN: 978-1-68515-208-6

All honor and glory to my Lord and my God,
Jesus Christ.
Thank You for my parents, who recognized
the importance of sharing the gift of faith with me.
Thank You for my three beautiful and gifted children,
Pio, Mary, and (Solis) Veronica. It is my prayer that
these three, who You have given to me, Father,
be protected and fed by You and, in turn,
continue to serve You by living out the gift of faith.
Thank You for my sisters and brothers.
Thank You for the people you have put on my path
that help bring me to life.
Thank You for extending me a tab and Your patience,
mercy, and gentle kindness when it goes unpaid.
To one of the most beautiful souls I have ever met,
Angie May. I am still convinced that you are an angel.
God smiles every moment He gazes upon you.
I love you.

CONTENTS

INTRODUCTION

In today's world, living up to Christian principles seems nearly impossible. Perhaps this is not the case for all, but it certainly is for me. I have an intuitive suspicion that if you have picked up this book, you may share in my struggle. My heart wants to follow the example of how to live set forth by Christ, yet I am torn between living in the world while trying to remain unstained by it. Sometimes I feel like I am riding a horse with a head at both ends that is running in opposite directions, with my head panning left to right in an attempt to decide which way to look and which direction to ride off to. It is exhausting!

It was not that long ago that my home was "the spot." Family, friends, and neighbors were always dropping by for a visit. I followed what I believed was social protocol. I dated for a few years, got engaged, and then married a year later. Shortly thereafter, we began to have children. Our home was filled with laughter and the sounds of busy feet and delightful interactions. There was hardly a Sunday when we would not immerse our senses in the aroma of a pot of sauce slowly cooking the meatballs on the kitchen stove. Dad and Mom lived right around the corner, and their lights were always on and the front door never locked. Life was good.

Fast-forward ten years, and you would have thought that an assassin under the cover of darkness had breached the front door of my life. The pictures started to fall off the shelves, the color began to fade, and what once felt like a full and rich life had all of a sudden become cold, dark, damp, and lonely. I was divorced and renting an apartment by myself for the first time in a long time. I was no longer waking up in a home with my children in their rooms. I had made some pretty serious choices that were the beginning of a painful and destructive journey. What happened to this man who felt like he had all that he ever wanted?

I awoke one day to a beeping sound and a feeling in my chest that I had never felt before. The beeping was a monitor, and the pressure I was experiencing was life support. The first words I heard were "Don't try to breathe. The machine is breathing for you."

I began to unleash intense anguish and proceeded to rip the tubes out of my body. Someone must have sedated me because the next thing I knew, I was waking up again, this time handcuffed to my bed. There is not much that I remember of that particular moment, but I do remember asking, "How did you find me?" I knew that I had just attempted suicide and should have had plenty of time to die since no one would have likely come looking for me for at least a day (this should have been more than enough time to succumb to the number of pills that I had taken just prior to climbing into bed in my apartment around noon on that fateful day). Someone responded, "You were in a bar." In my mind, that was impossible because I do not drink, so I never really went to bars.

I was soon after released from the hospital and needed answers. How did my foolproof plan fail? I needed to retrace my steps and visit the bar where I allegedly was discovered. I was convinced an angel must have plucked me from my bed. Did God spare my life? I needed to know. When I walked inside the bar, the bartender turned white as if he had seen a ghost. I asked him if he recognized me, and he immediately responded with the story from that day. Apparently, I had walked in, sat at the bar, and requested a drink. Within seconds of consuming the alcohol, I went into a coma and collapsed onto the patron at my side. He said I was airlifted to the hospital within minutes, which is where I eventually came to.

This was the first of four attempts at suicide in a very short period of time. After the fourth attempt, I awoke one morning behind a beautiful window made of bulletproof glass. This time, the first words I heard were "Welcome to Greystone." I was the newest resident of the state's notorious psychiatric facility. I turned and looked at my roommate, who was moaning over and over, "Get me out of here. Get me out of here. Get me out of here."

I looked at him and said, "I'm just here visiting someone." The truth is I was scared as hell. I was still willing to lie to myself, and I had no idea if and when I would ever get to go home. It seemed like the unknown created more anxiety than everything else combined. I remember laughing out loud and asking myself, "What happened to me? I used to be the happiest guy in the world, and now I am looking out the window of a psych ward."

There were a few things for certain: I was intent on dying, and I had come to learn that I was not very good at it, so I might as well try to live. Can we all agree that I had reached my rock bottom? How much closer can we get without actually being dead? This was actually great news as now the only direction to go was up. I learned that perception is everything. Taking a look back on my life, I can describe it as either filled with opportunities to give up or moments that made me better. The choice was mine. Which one would I choose to see myself as: victim or victor? My life was never really perfect, my attitude was never really that great, and my perception of it all was clear; I was broken. While I lay facedown, ear-deep in metaphorical mud that was absorbing me with its death grip, I heard the sound of a gun signaling the start of the race. The choice was mine: rise or die. Ready or not, I was now on my journey toward redemption.

CHAPTER ONE
The Broken Christian

W hat does today's Christian look like? The truth is, I am sure that one hundred Christians would give one hundred different answers. I am Catholic, and in my own family, it seems that there are several different versions of what it means to live out our Catholic Christian faith in our families and in our public life. I grew up in a traditional Catholic family. As children, we all went to church together. The boys dressed in suits and ties, and the girls dressed in full-length modest dresses. When we went to church, our shoes were polished and our hair combed. My sisters and mother each wore a veil, as it was part of Catholic tradition for a woman to cover her head during Mass; the church at large has long since relaxed this particular practice. So has the practice of men wearing suits and ties to church been mostly abandoned, among many other rituals and mandates.

The term "old school" is still used today to describe someone who maintains a way of life or ideals that changing times have seemed to relax in younger generations. Even for our generation growing up in the seventies and eighties, our family was considered "old school." Honestly speaking, I believe if someone were to come back from the dead who attended a Catholic Mass one hundred years ago, I am not sure they would believe they were standing in a Catholic church. That is how unrecognizable the celebration of the Mass has become in the last fifty to one hundred years. Unless this person was actually in a church built in the late 1800s and early 1900s, they may not believe they were actually even standing in a Catholic church at all.

The reason I lead with this thought is that even though we as Catholics may not have been alive long enough to witness the drastic departure from "old school" Catholic rituals and religious practices, its effect upon us is very real and may bear some responsibility for the struggles we endure in our lives that make it hard to be a practicing Catholic in good standing with the church and, ultimately, with God. Is there a connection between how we practice our faith and what the liturgy of the Mass is today compared to what it once was even fifty to sixty years ago? Most of my family members who were alive in the seventies are still alive today, and most still call themselves Catholic. Yet, somehow, we seem to live different Catholic lives. This is not an indication of one living a good life while the other a bad—just different. Just like traditions and cultures vary around the world, in my little world, it sometimes feels like we are more strangers than brothers and sisters in Christ. This is not strictly the case in my immediate family, but more so across the wider Christian community.

If I were to give myself a classification, I would describe myself as a middle-of-the-road Catholic. I attend

Mass weekly and try to follow typical Catholic norms. I still say my prayers before meals, I try to get to Mass on holy days, and I get my ashes on Ash Wednesday, etc. So what is the problem? Why do I feel the need to write this book and relate to people? As I have affirmed in my introduction, something went drastically wrong. Whatever the details and reasons, today I am a divorced man whose current Christian life feels incomplete. The choices I have made (and sometimes still make) leave me in a spiritual condition that some might call disordered with God and his church. In other words, God desires order, and right now, my life is mismatched and slightly disjointed. While striving to remain a Catholic and one who is in good standing with God's holy church, I have begun the task of utilizing the methods and means offered by His church to restore order to my life. Hopefully I can find a peace that resembles the life I thought I enjoyed at one time, but this time in a manner that is lasting and holistic with the woman that I love and renewed relationships with family and friends.

In today's world, the narrative is "do you." It is that simple. Do what makes you happy. This is more than just a narrative; it is a modern-day creed and a new way of life. It is a way of life that creeps up on you and eventually becomes you. As for Catholicism, there is a sort of spiritual science behind it. If you want to live a happy life, there is a formula you must follow. It is when we as humans begin to deviate from the prescription Christ has set before us that our lives begin to fall apart. This is not necessarily a matter of fault; it is a matter of ownership. It is my personal opinion that very little of what has happened to us in our lives is solely of our own doing. I understand that some responsibility is on us to fashion a healthy life for ourselves, some is on the outside influences responsible for caring for and protecting us, and I believe the largest portion of accountability belongs to the leaders of the Catholic Church, both past and present.

This is not an attempt to find a scapegoat for my problems. I believe the reality of the situation is that church leaders have been "asleep at the wheel" and have been steering us away from the very happiness that awaits us when we live a true Catholic Christian life. It is important to identify the problem before trying to find the solution. In order to determine who bears the burden of procuring a Christian God-fearing and God-loving society, it will be helpful in figuring out who bears what responsibility for the breakdown of the Christian family and the interior life of a Christian. For me, make that specifically a Catholic Christian family. This would ultimately assist in understanding what part I played in the dismantling of my own life and what I can and must do to unravel the damage I have caused toward myself and attempt to repair it.

We need to stay grounded throughout this process by remembering where we are at this moment in life. It is less important how we got here and much more important to get to where we are going; ultimately, that destination is heaven. In the meantime, there is a certain happiness that comes with following God's will that we can experience in this life as we continue to grow in holiness and even more so in the midst of pain and trials that we may come face-to-face with.

Do you feel that you have you deviated from your faith? What obstacles can you identify in your life that you can see have come between you and God, disrupting a full communion with Him? Jesus knew how far off track our lives would become. He quite often spoke about lost sheep that know their Shepherd's voice. That Shepherd knows our voice too. He knows us intimately. Christ has declared Himself "The Good Shepherd." This is not because we are animals to Him. It is because our nature causes us to run when we are scared and wander while we feed. We are vulnerable creatures that He wants to care for and that He loves dearly. He knew that we would stray from His flock. He is currently searching us out. If you have not found the Lord, is it because He has not been able to find you? We are on the run. He is in pursuit of us, calling us each by name. Hopefully we grow weary of sinning and stop running. Our Lord's prayer to His Father was that "none of those whom You have given me may be lost" (John 17:12).

What will it take to get us to stop running, and when will the weight of our cross be too much to bear? There are many reasons why I have been "on the run" in my life. I think it boils down to this expression: "The spirit is willing, but the flesh is weak" (Matthew 26:41). My human nature is divided into two parts; I have two masters, and as Christ has said, "Man cannot serve two masters" (Matthew 6:24). God is my master, and my flesh is the other master. He created us with a soul that desires Him, and that soul is dressed in flesh that desires the things of the flesh. That is not necessarily as sinful as it sounds, but it can easily become so.

Nearly everything we do in the flesh serves the flesh: we eat and drink, go to work, and exercise. We go fishing and sailing, skydiving and swimming. We have barbecues and go to amusement parks. We lie down in our beds, wake up, and spend time with our families and friends. The list can go on endlessly. Every day, we bathe our senses in the pleasures of this world. Sometimes we might even take a hike and think *What a spiritual experience!* Yes, for our eyes! We are indeed spiritual creatures who enjoy good spiritual experiences. There is absolutely nothing wrong with that or even our nature. Now imagine if while we are on that hike and we come to this beautiful mountain top that overlooks the earth for miles and we say to ourselves, "What a spiritual experience! I must go tell everyone I know about this spot and share this with all who would love to experience it with me!" We have what we would call a communal gathering. That is precisely what our attendance at Mass is, except this view is a front row seat to the personal awesomeness of God, where we give glory to Him for His holy sacrifice and free gift of salvation and redemption.

That outdoor mountaintop view was spiritual indeed; it was the voice of God calling you and me to Him. He wants us to discover Him and glorify Him after we rid ourselves of fleshly obsessions and begin to tap into the spiritual aspect of our nature. He is calling us to stop serving our flesh and start tending to it. He wants us to use our flesh and our spirits to serve Him. We are called to glorify our God with our whole being. We need to let the Good Shepherd catch up to us. He has many others to find as well. We need to join Him in searching for others as well. It is difficult to do this when we feel lost and are struggling to understand who we are. That is what I was noticed about myself. I could not bear to look at myself any longer. What I was seeing was ugliness, shame, and unworthiness. I used to believe that I was a moderately attractive man. I know that there have been times when my behavior may have been unattractive, but as for looks, I was at least "okay." What are we saying when we find ourselves or others attractive? To me, what we are saying is "I am drawn to you." Yes, if I look into the mirror and find myself attractive, I am saying to myself, "I am drawn to you." I think I know why we find Christ unattractive, which causes us to run from Him. He is bloody and full of mortal wounds. This can be a bit scary. We treat Him like He is a serial killer in pursuit of us, but the reality is that it is we who have mortally wounded Him. He is chasing after us, crying out, "I want to forgive you! I will forgive you!"

Is attraction really about our looks? The truth is we do not like looking at wounds because they turn our stomachs. The greater the wound, the more we look away. We enjoy looking at things that are desirable. We close our eyes when the flesh is mutilated and disfigured. The only wounds we typically enjoy looking at are our own. We even like showing them to others. We want sympathy and attention. We want to be cared for. We want someone to listen to our stories of how we became wounded and tell us we are going to be all right.

It is not until we begin to love someone when we fail to see his or her scars anymore; something inside of them becomes visible. We do not even realize that what we are beginning to see is their soul. When we love someone so purely, we are actually seeing what is inside of him or her. We are no longer distracted by what sin has done to the flesh. We are no longer seeing man or woman, white or black, old or young. We are only seeing brother or sister. What we are seeing is a child of God. I believe the truth is when our deepest love is shared with someone, it is a truly nonsexual experience. Think of most of the people who you love. Sex is the furthest thing from your mind. We actually have to become carnal and of the flesh to procreate. God willed it to be so, but most of our earthly interactions are nonphysical (in the sexual sense), even with our spouse.

When we can begin to see our flesh for exactly what it is, we can start to use it in order to serve our God. As I have said previously, when a husband and wife use their flesh to serve God, they can create a life that can eventually grow up to know, love, and serve his or her God. If we can reserve our carnal desires for the use of serving God, we can begin to repair what is broken, namely our relationship with our Father. Jesus used His flesh to serve His Father, whom He already intimately knew and loved, even unto death. Maybe when we can learn to see past the flesh, we will actually see Christ in the Eucharist, where we will find healing. I want Him to heal me. Most of us will never experience the blessing of a miraculous healing. Most of us will have to experience the pain of correction. It will take hard work and honesty. It will take time and patience. We need to measure our growth and realize that we are being drawn to the most attractive person who ever lived. If we think that we are or someone we know is magnetic, then imagine that Christ is gravity. He is forever drawing us to Him. When we stop running from Christ and draw nearer to Him, we can begin the process of redemption.

CHAPTER TWO
Redemption

I have always equated redemption with salvation. The two just seem to go hand in hand. In matters of our faith, these may be two of the most important words to take with us into the next life. Considering the fact that we have not crossed over, yet let us apply them to this life for starters. We are still clothed in flesh. Our hearts are beating, and our lungs are still expanding and contracting. We are alive! Now the question becomes "Are we living?" I needed to learn how to do that, and my guess is that you do too.

As I have difficultly shared earlier, I am living a post-suicidal life today. Upon arriving home from the hospital for the last time, I had a decision to make. Do I want to keep dying or start living? There were warning signs that I was previously more interested in dying, one being that I began to give my belongings away to friends and family. This should have been a giant red flag to those who love me. In my mind, I was convinced that no one loved me and I was irredeemable. I was trying to sneak out the "back door of life," like I was quietly leaving the party. I actually witnessed this several years later, and I did not pick up on it. That is how clever we can be when we are in a very dark place. A friend of mine attempted to give me something of his that was special to him, and his wife stopped him. A few weeks later, he made an attempt on his life. He was saved.

By the time I had reached the point of no return, I felt empty. I was missing vital elements to my being. I had no self-esteem, no self-love, no self-worth, no vision of a tomorrow, and no selfless acts left in me. In the final moment, I had no thought of others and how this would affect them. Just prior, I had convinced myself that this was for the best and everyone would be better off without me in the world. I did more than just run out of gas. If I were a car, all that would have been left was the frame. The engine, the exhaust, the windows, the seats, the steering wheel, the glove box, the carpeting, and all four tires were completely gone in my mind. I was unrecognizable, undrivable, and therefore worthless and better described as scrap. I must warn all who are reading this that if you ever encounter someone who is irrationally feeling this way, as I was, never pour fuel on the fire by calling it a pity party. Do not call them selfish or insult them in some other way. Do not say, "Snap out of it." For some people, the process of emptying that I described happens in mere seconds. For me, it happened much slower over time. The best thing you can do for someone who is suffering with the thought of futility is to spend time with him or her and talk to them. Remind this person of how many people love them and find value in them. If you are able to be by their side, then do it. Oftentimes, the feeling passes fairly quickly and they may start to feel better, but it will likely return, so keep in contact as regularly as you can.

What if this person is you, and maybe you are not as empty as I was, but you feel like you are getting there? I cannot tell you what to do, but I can tell you what I did. As with anyone in life who is dishonest, I needed to stop lying to myself. The irrational thoughts kept coming. I needed to dispute them and ask myself, "Is this true? Am I really unlovable?" The clear and obvious answer was "No!" There were plenty of people who loved me. If needed, I would write the names of these people on a paper in front of me so I could see it for myself. A new irrational thought would come through my head: "You are a failure." Some of these lies seem so true because we feel like we have not gotten as far as we would have liked to in life or have suffered some sort of setback. I needed to get some feedback from people I loved and respected: "I feel like I have failed. Do you see me as a failure?" Ten times out of ten, someone you love and who loves you will show you multiple ways in which you have succeeded. They will help you define success and what it looks like for you. They will remind you to stop comparing yourself to others and set your own attainable goals and help you to achieve each of your own miniature successes.

Not everyone reading this has a strong network of friends and family. Some people literally have no one left to support them. There are so many people in your community who are ready, willing, and able to lock arms with you and get your legs working again. They are experienced in social and mental health matters and are qualified to not only get your legs working but to help you to run again. Even people with families would benefit from community resources. One of the first obstacles I encountered coming home from the psychiatric hospital was the fear of going outside my home. My irrational thought was if I went outside or went into town, I was going to mess up somehow and get brought back to the hospital. Being in the hospital environment was quite traumatic for me, and I never wanted to go back, so I thought if I just stayed in my house, I would be safe.

I do not quite remember how much time had passed before I got an envelope in the mail from a local non-profit initiative explaining that they received my name from my local parish as someone who may benefit from their self-help course that was beginning soon. Tell me that was not God extending His healing hand out to me! The answer I gave was clear and quick: "Nope." My response would have been "Absolutely!" if the classes were held at my home. Since it required me to venture outdoors, I had to respectfully decline. God did not give up on me though. About a month later, they reached out again. This time my irrational fears were beginning to subside, and I thought, *What have I got to lose?* The name of the initiative was Pathways to Prosperity.

When I began to attend the twenty-six week course, it was very awkward at first. My thought was *What if I see someone I know?* It took a little while to get past the superficial worries and get down to work. It required two hours of my life once a week. I find it rather humorous that I worried about what other people would think when I was trying to help myself. First order of business: stop worrying about what other people are going to think. They were likely feeling just as uncomfortable, and we were all there to better our situations.

Although Pathways reached out to my church for a name, they were not affiliated with my church. They were a completely secular nondenominational organization and seldom spoke about God. I would not say that they never did because when we learned about our personal resources, spirituality was one of them. There was no doubt in my mind, though, that I was experiencing the hand of God. One thing was for certain: it took a measure of humility to be a part of this group. Initially, as I have described, it was quite embarrassing having to admit that I needed help and that something went wrong with my life. That sense of humility began to change over time. I began to experience humility mixed with gratitude that eventually became a new word: "humbletude." The outpouring of love and care I was receiving from my community greatly humbled me. There were so many people who came out to offer assistance to someone in need of a helping hand. What was even more amazing was that some of the volunteers were from previous classes who had successfully completed the course and were now giving back.

I found something over the duration of time I spent working on myself. I was beginning to redeem parts of me that I thought were all but lost for good. I began to not only get some color back to my face, but also to my life. I found out that I am worthy of love and capable of loving others in a healthier way. I realized that it is okay to love myself. I began to enjoy being in my own company and sitting in front of a mirror without despising who was looking back at me. None of this happened overnight. I was on a path to success, and I will continue to journey on it until I die. I recommend you to be leery of those who promise overnight success. This is an oxymoron. Success is a climb, not a fall. It requires dedication, devotion, and good old-fashioned hard work. More often than not, there will be setbacks and crushing pain. The most compelling moments in movies are when the hero gets knocked down, it appears that all is lost, and they are about to be counted out. All of a sudden, with every fiber of their being, they begin to twitch and then move, and then, ever so exhaustedly, they begin to rise again, ultimately to a bloody, sweaty victory.

This actually has happened in real life. Movie directors have used this concept to inspire viewers, but there is someone that *has* actually overcome all adversity and completed every challenge, proving that it is possible to rise from the deepest depths and beat the greatest odds. That person is our Savior and Redeemer Jesus Christ. His cross is our sins, the weight of which crushed Him to the earth, tearing through Him with hellish fury from the moment His passion began. In one day, His world became a merciless thrashing of violence unlike anything a human being had ever experienced before or has ever since. Between each moment he was tortured, His holy, innocent wounds began to heal just to be torn open again, this time with increased vengeance and wrath. He was robbed of all dignity, stripped of all humanity, and divested of every inch of majesty and countenance. He was brought to absolute nothingness, and all anyone dared to do was watch and cry. Christ's passion went on for hours and was so frightful that I am sure even Satan and his demon angels were terrified. What was by every standard and measure an absolute defeat was in fact the greatest victory ever achieved by a human being. Jesus had successfully opened the gates of heaven again. His will and determination was so indestructible that He achieved what no other man could have endured and overcome. Although He is God, He accomplished this as a man. He used no special power and performed no miracle from the moment of His arrest until His death on the cross. He did this for us to show us that it is humanly possible to overcome all adversity that will ever come our way, and there were two words that sum it all up. He believed we were *redeemable* and *worthy* of being saved. If Our Lord found such value in me that He would endure such misery even if it were just for me, what can I do for myself to help myself that would not require even a fraction of that self-discipline? All of these new insights were demanding something of me. It was time for change.

CHAPTER THREE

Self-Aware
and Ready to Act

One of the beauties of being a human is that we are aware of our existence. We have the ability to evaluate our behaviors and make corrections where it is necessary. The entire mission of my life is to form a deeper bond with God. I find no greater purpose to my existence than to take the broken view I have had of myself and develop a healthier perception of who I really am. Once I am able to observe myself correctly, I can make the necessary changes that are essential to cultivating my relationship with my Father.

Something I have learned on my journey of recovery is how to describe myself; for instance, I was not depressed but rather I had depression. If I had a cold or a flu, you would not call me a cold or a flu. For a man who struggles with drug addiction, he is not a drug addict; he is a person with a chemical addiction or a substance use disorder. I have spent a lot of time sitting in on community awareness meetings, and I was glad to see that in the medical and professional world, the way we speak about other human beings and ourselves is starting to gain more importance.

Ironically, I was watching a particular show on television where a certain doctor interviews people and then exploits their defects while stroking his own ego, and he was tearing apart a woman for wanting to have another baby at her age. If I can correctly recall, he asked her (paraphrased), "Why the hell would you want to have another child when you have two Down syndrome babies already?" Whether it was one baby or two, I do not remember, but what I found shocking was his reference to the woman's children as "Down syndrome babies." With all of the discussion in the medical field about how to speak to people, this person, whose credentials I would love to send to a forensic laboratory, should have known better. The babies he was referring to are actually *two children with* Down syndrome. What he did—and I am sure we all have done many times—is define ourselves by our weakest moments or worst attributes.

When we learn how to become more thoughtful of how we think and speak, we can begin to heal. I needed to do a lot of that. There were so many untruths that I believed about myself. The lies I was convinced of began when I was young. I remember one particular instance when I was about eight or nine. I was wearing a black T-shirt that had the words "THINK BIG" printed in bold white letters on the front. I felt cool and smart. I am sure I was not even certain at the time what the phrase meant, but it sounded good, and on top of that, none of my siblings had a shirt that had writing on it, so I felt special. In a moment, that would all change when I bruised the ego of a particular grown-up who was "near and dear" to my family. I thought he would laugh, but maybe I should have known better. Being the little wise guy that I was, I made a playful remark at his expense, and he tore into me with words that affected me deeper than I had then realized. The reason I remember this story is because of how he used the words on my shirt to humiliate and degrade me in front of others who were present, ultimately ripping the shirt to pieces right from my body. His assault dragged on and on. He was not going to stop until he felt comfortable that I would never make that mistake again.

It may be obvious to the reader that this man was an abuser, and, in time, he would successfully dismantle any healthy sense of self that I had. Being allowed to go on for years unchecked compounded this abusive environment. It did not last forever, although I always believed that I would die as part of his personal property. He passed away when I was in my late twenties, but the damage was more than done. I was always a quite forgiving person, and I even confronted him while he was still alive so I could hear him say the words I longed to hear. The best he could give me was "If I hurt you, I'm sorry." That was so big but yet so fragmented. He did not exactly take ownership of his behavior but rather put it back on me to decide if I was injured by him or not. I offered him words of forgiveness and felt a ton of weight lifted from my heart. I was brave enough and man enough to confront the man who took just about every unique quality from me, replacing it with shame, insecurity, guilt, brokenness, doubt, disbelief, distrust, and every defeated ingredient I needed to be his well-behaved servant.

My forgiveness offered to him helped me but only carried me so far. I began to live an independent life and finally started to enjoy the things that "normal" people do like go on dates and get married and start a family. We have arrived now at the period of my life described in my introduction. Sometimes we let words fly and react to others thoughtlessly. We do not mean anything by it, and it is easily corrected with a little thoughtful conversation. These types of careless words are normally situational and not indicative of a deeper problem. However, due to all the repressed emotions and irrationality I carried with me, his words ran deep like cancer attached to each of my cells. The more I tried to live a normal life, the more my mind was trying to deal with my childhood trauma, so they started to manifest, and in a big way. What I thought was my ascension out of the abyss of my former life began to appear to be a nosedive back.

I needed to go back to that dark place and find someone—that someone was an eight-year-old boy who was wearing a shirt with "THINK BIG" written on it. He was stuck in that moment, and only I could find him and bring him out. The only way to achieve this successfully was to confront the lies and the pain and replace it with a new narrative. A new narrative ,however, is not simply a new set of words. It requires empathy, understanding, and a new story. It requires honesty and hard work. If my house looks like that of a hoarder, I cannot just say, "It is a clean house now." I must take the time and sort out the good from the bad and develop a sense of organization and discipline. I was hoarding beliefs about myself that someone else told me to believe. I was incapable of discarding them, and in some strange way, I accepted the mental dialogue and found comfort in it. If I accepted that I was broken, I could excuse my unhealthy behavior. If I was broken, I could be more accepting of others who are broken. All of the words that go along with this skewed way of thinking worked for me. For instance: "I can consider myself disabled." "I am damaged goods." "I have a lot of baggage." "I am faking it through life." It took me a while to realize that *some other squirrel had stored his nuts in my head.*

One of the most impactful lessons I learned during the twenty-six-week self-help course I took was how to use my strengths to balance out my weaknesses. Of the eleven personal resources each person possesses, eight of mine were fragmented and three were still intact. The three that I felt most confident in were my social skills, my friends and family support, and my spiritual strength. I find it easy talking with others and always am ready to make a stranger a friend. I had fairly strong ties with family and friends who had assured me I could always reach out before ever throwing it all away again, and my faith in God was deep. Between these three distinct qualities, I realized my success was truly within my own reach. My confidence level began to increase, and I was surely clever enough to execute a new plan. One of the first wishes on my bucket list of healthy living was to be able to sleep at night without the use of medicine. Using my social skill, I reached out to a loving family member who I knew was always ready to listen. He shared with me a quite similar struggle he had experienced and had the perfect book for me to read. It was called *Achieving*

Peace of Heart by S. J. Lewis Delmage Irala Narciso. He mailed it to me, and after reading it, I have kept it close to my bedside ever since until this day. Right on page one, Rev. Irala writes in black and white:

> We should of course bear in mind that the happiness of this life is necessarily limited and imperfect. But though we are, in this book, seeking no earthly utopia, we must admit that much of our "unhappiness" is self-made and unnecessary, much of it the outcome of seeking a false "happiness."

From what I understood him to be saying, *I needed to stop looking into a broken mirror and thinking my eyes were bad*. People and things around me may have failed me as a child, but I did not fail myself, and I needed to stop looking for people to blame and start taking ownership of my present and future vision. I was only going to look back into my past if there was a lesson I could draw from to improve my current situation or to help someone else. I discovered that reading and learning something new made me exhausted, and I further noticed I would fall asleep while reading my new book without having taken any medicine. I was ecstatic to share with the loving family member who sent me the book that changes were taking place and my faith was starting to fill in a giant hole in my life. I was beginning to find peace! True and lasting peace comes from a relationship with Christ. Up until then, my god was my antianxiety medication. I put my trust in it and felt lost without it. As a point of fact, nights that I had tried sleeping without it, I found myself up all night. I find it mildly humorous how Satan will even use the science of medicine that God has given us to convince us that we do not need God. Actually, God has designed this system so well that Satan uses this genius design to convince us that we are completely capable of thriving in this life without God's assistance.

The prescription I was taking to help me sleep was given to me prior to any hospital stays. It was even given to me during my time at the state hospital. I became so heavily reliant upon it that it likely contributed to my difficulty functioning with my daily activities. Subsequent to my release from the psychiatric hospital, I was approved for permanent disability. The doctors, after reviewing my case and the level of diagnosed severe post-traumatic stress disorder and chronic major depressive disorder, were convinced my condition was permanent. I was directly told that I would never have to work again and all that I needed to do was report in every three years and let them know that my condition had not changed. I am not going to lie, that was music to the ears of someone who saw himself as broken, but as I began the ardent work of improving my condition and *no longer used other people's words to describe myself*, the prospect of never working again began to sound utterly ridiculous. Receiving the help offered to me by the State Disability Bureau was actually the exact thing I needed at the time.

As I mentioned earlier, of my eleven personal resources, my finances were suffering and therefore creating stress and imbalance. So to have the opportunity to take a break from breadwinning for a period of time was vitally necessary. The state even paid for me to enroll in schooling. Education, although I did not consider myself uneducated, was another resource I could stand to improve. I was so moved by the tremendous empathy and generosity that I wrote the state's care advocate a letter thanking her for her kind consideration with a promise that I would excel in the training. I completed the schooling top in my class.

Things were beginning to change in my life that I began to have a problem with the word "disabled" as it did not quite fit who I began to now see in the mirror. New challenge: convince the disability board that I was no longer in need of their assistance, but that I was truly grateful for the help while I was ill. We eventually worked it out, and I nervously severed ties with them. I was standing, for now, on my own two feet again, and it was a strange feeling considering I was a grown man, divorced with three children who heavily relied on my competence to care for them. By now, I had completed the self-help course and the state-financed schooling, and I was completely unsure how I was going to earn enough of a living to provide as I used to for my family and myself. My resources were gaining in quantity and quality, and I now had a new loving partner who, as a true friend, saw me through every stage of my rehabilitation and immersion to a world that I had once attempted to leave behind but now gratefully and eagerly embraced. I began to realize that much of my new happiness was always there to be shared in; what was once missing was a healthy realization of what life was about: *the inhale and the exhale.* It is always a give and take.

A poem I wrote during this period, "The Fruit Tree in the Broken Pot":

Oh water of truth, I yearn to contain your wisdom…
Oh soil of love, don't dry out in my midst. For I long to be rooted and firm in stature…
But the pot I call "Me" has been damaged by storm.
I rejoice, as grace like the rain follows the veins of my leaves of yearning…
Across the stems of my attempts, down the stalk of my convictions…
Riding the roots of determination to be absorbed by the fibers of my being.
I drink, and then I thirst.

This pot I call "Me" is my image of self.
My image of self is of one who is broken.
My image of self is of one who can't deal.
My image of self is that I won't make it.
My image of self is one that's not real.

Oh Master of Clay, lay Your hands on my being.
Reshape and repair what I may have chosen to destroy.
There are holes in my walls that slow down my growth, and the gifts in my life escape through my sides.
Plaster and bond with a new understanding. Plaster and bond with a love of myself. For until I love me, I will struggle to fully love others.

When spring arrives, my buds of self-worth will sprout.
Others will see the beauty that I see in myself. Before

long, I will bear much fruit of success for others to enjoy under the comfort of my outstretched branches.

I am strong. I am loyal. I love who I am. I do not fear the fracture.
My pot is in Good Hands.

CHAPTER FOUR
The Cultural Dance

This is where life gets tricky. Our Lord desires for us to extract ourselves from the snares of earthly distractions and set our sights on Him. What does this mean and encompass? In Romans 12:1–3, Saint Paul writes:

> I beseech you therefore, brethren, by the mercy of God, that you present your bodies a living sacrifice, holy, pleasing unto God, your reasonable service. And be not conformed to this world; but be reformed in the newness of your mind, that you may prove what is the good, and the acceptable, and the perfect will of God. For I say, by the grace that is given me, to all that are among you, not to be more wise than it behoveth to be wise, but to be wise unto sobriety, and according as God hath divided to everyone the measure of faith.

This may be the biggest challenge for a Christian: "How do I exist in a secular society while maintaining my integrity of faith?" There are plenty of groups and sects of people who are quite comfortable living their orthodox or puritan way of life. They limit their interactions with the rest of the world to maintain a tradition that preserves coherence of their faith-based life. We see this quite often in what some refer to as ultra-conservative religious groups like Orthodox Jews, the Amish, Mormons, Orthodox Catholic/Christian, certain Hindu, Buddhists, and Muslims, among several others. Truth be told, no matter what religion one clings to, there are always going to be those who try to practice that belief in utter detail. In most cases, it may be easy to spot someone who follows a conformist lifestyle by the way they are dressed. For women, this would typically be full-length attire and in some cases headdresses and very little skin revealed. Men can be a little more difficult to pick out, as men do not have the same wardrobe demands as women do in most cases. Depending on the religious group, some men may be required to wear particular headwear. This is where I begin to challenge the leaders of my Catholic faith.

As in other areas of my life, I experience a lack of balance, and as I try to understand what the Lord is asking of me here, I would sum it up with "stay on the balance beam." As a child, I always looked forward to the times of year when we got to do gymnastics for our physical education class. One of my weakest skill sets, oddly enough, was the balance beam. We have all tried it as a child—on a curb, on a low brick wall, or some other structure that challenged our ability to balance. Most times, it ended with a rapid shuffling of the feet and off I went. The challenge I place before the church leaders is to be more attentive to the need for balance in the lives of the church's faithful. As in the case of the balance beam, balance is not something that comes naturally to humans, or everyone would be a master of the beam. I am not merely speaking of walking without falling down. What I am referring to is the acrobatics we need to do while on the beam. It needs to be taught by those who have mastered the art of it and learned by everyone whose life depends on it. Show me one person who would not benefit from balance, and I will agree that it is not a vital skill that every man and woman must learn.

Most things that I can think of are engineered symmetrically. When I put on a shirt, each half of its design matches. One arm is not longer than the other. The legs of a chair are of equal length. Even a book has a front cover and a back cover. Perhaps without realizing it, we rely very heavily on balance. Our existence would be rather burdensome without it. Is this not what Jesus is trying to convey to us? If so, then how can we master the burden of balance so we can successfully remain in the world while failing to be defined by the world?

First, we need to consider where society gets it wrong, and immediately we can look to mainstream popular culture. That is a fancy way of saying, "Look no further than movies, television, and magazines." Who, what, and where are we getting our influences from? I can honestly say I have never ventured out in public and noticed that the person next to me was wearing an outfit made of raw meat. As a matter of fact, never was someone wearing cooked meat, cereal, pasta, or any other type of food source as clothing. I will tell you where I did see it: on television. If you personally have never seen this, you may be wondering what kind of weird channel I watch. This is no special programming; it is mainstream media. Television may be the single worst offender. It seems that there is an ever-increasing intention to slaughter morality and decency in television and the entertainment industry.

This world that we live in was created by God but has been hijacked by Satan for some time now. So it should come as no surprise to us that we need to be cautious of what we are consuming. There should be no doubt in our mind that every bit of our secular society has been overrun by the devil. Even our religious tracts have been forcefully under siege. Have we not heard enough horror stories of vile men who have breached the walls of our sanctuaries under the guise of being priests and what dreadful acts they have perpetrated upon innocent children? Are we not all aware of the violent Muslim extremists raping and beheading innocent men, women, and children? This is not balance. This is absolute and complete darkness.

Every time a new extreme is introduced, it has made the old extreme look middle-of-the-road. This is a ploy. We have seen this in music, fashion, and entertainment. There is no attempt to disguise immorality anymore. These are a few examples of the programming menus being offered as mindless entertainment:

—*Temptation Island* ("anything goes" dating game, one of several)
—*90 Day Fiancé* (must get proposed to in ninety days)

—*Naked and Afraid* (man and woman surviving naked)

—*Labor of Love* (a woman wants a baby and must find her right man)

—*Ex on the Beach* (dating game with innuendo title—anything goes)

These are obvious examples of blatant immorality in television. All you need to see is a commercial promoting the show to be inadvertently pushed a little farther out into the abyss. Now when your program returns and a little off-color humor is used or a sexual innuendo is made, it does not appear so dreadful anymore. Think of how the ocean appears to push you to shore, but just before you reach land, it siphons you a little further out. Before it is realized, you are lost at sea.

I watched a lot of television and was no different than anyone else. I laughed at the dirty jokes; I did not turn the channel. Some things even made me disgusted, which means I found them disgusting, yet I continued to watch. I would justify it as mindless entertainment and "bubble gum for the brain," as they say. I began to see television for what it is to me, a pure sugar mental diet rotting my brain. What is referred to as reality television is actually the furthest thing from real, yet it begins to shape our culture. Fashions are introduced through these shows that begin to dictate what you and I should be wearing in order to stay relevant. Family life is shaped for us in front of our eyes. Shows like *Shameless* indoctrinate us with what a godless family life looks like. We learn new lingo and begin to redefine what a true dynamic family is. Even in sports we have been bombarded with drama and indoctrination. To speak out against any of the errors will get a person cancelled very quickly in life.

What we are witnessing in our time are the very social errors of liberalism that Pope Leo XIII condemned in his encyclical *Rerum Novarum* in the late 1800s. Our leaders used to directly confront popular culture and address the errors of the times as did Pope Pius the IX in his encyclical *Syllabus of Errors*. I am confident that our brothers and sisters in Christ would greatly benefit from parental guidance that trains the faithful in matters of morality when it comes to our encounters with music, television, and movies as the church once offered these types of directives. Would we listen? I cannot answer this question; whether it is too late or we are too stubborn to take criticism remains unknown. Nonetheless, like many other things parents make children take, some sound moral advice should be given anyway.

If we find ourselves in need of change and desiring to mend broken mindsets and uneven paths in our life, then maybe developing a healthy conscience would benefit us. We need our church leaders to not give up on us. How can we develop balance between a wounded church and ourselves? We will explore these thoughts later, but we still have some unpacking of our own issues to deal with. While trying to put the pieces back together, I was challenged by a lack of support from others around me. It took me a little while to decipher who had my best interests at heart, and who had ulterior motives. I found one particular method used against me quite difficult to make sense of: Why were certain people avoiding me?

CHAPTER FIVE

Don't Let the Shun
Go Down on Me

Call it what you want—the shun, cold shoulder, or the ice treatment—most of the time, it does not work. As a person of faith who has made some wrong turns in life, I am well acquainted with being shunned. Catholics do not have exclusive rights to it. It is a global mechanism and is even used in homes between husbands and wives, parents and children, friends and coworkers. It is the fastest and easiest way to say so much without having to say anything at all, right? I am not so sure about that. Although it would likely be beneficial to explore all the ways shunning is used, the one that I would like to begin focusing on is the one that has been used on me the most, which is the "you are living in sin" shun. This encompasses all of the shunning that goes along with religious practices.

If we are going to be able to repair this unhealthy image of self that we have, it might help to recognize when someone is weaponizing a tool. Yes, you did read that correctly. Shunning is actually a tool and can be used for the good of mankind. The problem is most people do not understand this tool and end up hurting each other and making situations and relationships worse. Research the phrase "what the Bible says about shunning." You will find verse after verse that gives license to our friends and family to ignore us and shut us out. How many brothers have gone years without talking to each other? How many fathers and sons have done the same? It is not gender exclusive. *The problem with shunning someone is it can have the effect of a psychological grenade.*

I have said it before that it matters less how we got to our broken place and more how we are going to move forward. Does it matter if it is me or someone else that appears broken? I know someone who was in a homosexual relationship. They were getting ready to marry the person they were in a relationship with. I do not know of any mainstream religion that puts their blessing on this type of union. So by most religious standards, it is written in black and white that homosexuality is a sin and therefore one cannot enter heaven as such. It did not take long for all of the condemnation to start flying. Those who loved this person needed to make sure that he was aware of what God says about this type of lifestyle. The shunning followed shortly behind. What does the Bible say on this matter? I will take a passage from the same Douay Rheims Bible I have used in every other instance to keep the message throughout this book consistent. Scripture says in 1 Corinthians 9–10:

> Know you not that the unjust shall not possess the kingdom of God? Do not err: neither fornicators, nor idolaters, nor adulterers, Nor the effeminate, nor liers

with mankind, nor thieves, nor covetous, nor drunk-
ards, nor railers, nor extortioners, shall possess the
kingdom of God.

A person who claims to adhere to Catholicism cannot
argue that, according to the source of scripture used in
Catholic moral theology, this type of behavior is forbidden by God if it is our hope and goal to enter the kingdom of heaven. For the moment, let us pretend that
homosexuality is the only sin mentioned above. Now
let us stop pretending and realize that there are several
forbidden acts listed. The reason I will not address it
solely is because that is how we shape weapons. We
pick out the line that most fits our argument, and we
sharpen it and stab with it. If I am correct, murderers
are forbidden as well. There is more than one way to
skin a cat, and more than one way to kill a person. The
way I am alluding to is the killing of one's spirit. So
how do we correct someone's behavior without killing
them? There is another scripture that begins to address
this passage from Luke 6:42:

> Or how canst thou say to thy brother: Brother, let me
> pull the mote out of thy eye, when thou thyself seest
> not the beam in thy own eye? Hypocrite, cast first
> the beam out of thy own eye; and then shalt thou see
> clearly to take out the mote from thy brother's eye.

We may all be familiar with this passage from scripture,
as we may have needed to use it at times in our lives.
The word "mote" translates elsewhere to "splinter." In

no uncertain terms, Christ warns us that if we truly want to help another person out of their sinful ways, we must remove the large obstacle in our own life first that inhibits our ability to see well enough to help our neighbor whose faults may actually turn out to be far less offensive and sinful than our own. What Christ is telling us is that we should focus on our personal relationship with God that we may come to remove any obstacles of sin that prevent us from enjoying a full and rich relationship with Christ. How do we know exactly when that moment has come when the beam is finally removed? Two thoughts come to mind:

1) We will never know for sure.
2) We will know when it happens.

My guess is that it all boils down to relationships. When we develop a healthy relationship with someone, we learn to communicate with them in a way that is kind, respectful, thoughtful, and unselfish. In my life, I have had similar experiences of being shunned. Having gone through a divorce, I was already drawing negative attention from God-fearing people. Soon after I ended my marriage civilly, I met another woman who I found myself instantly attracted to. We exchanged numbers, communicated a few times with each other, and lost touch for several months. As fate would have it, we crossed paths again and were happily surprised to have reconnected. There are a few things to bear in mind: I had just gone through a divorce and a loss of several people and things in my life, and I was in a very dark and unhealthy place at this time in my life. Nevertheless, the young lady and I pursued a friendship, and over time, that friendship developed into a more emotional connection where we began to fall in love. I was still in the midst of dealing with a lot of my unresolved childhood trauma. The issues from my previous marriage were far from completely worked out, and I was running out of steam fast. If life had one more straw to place on my back, it was not going to be a good scene. That straw came soon enough when a close friend of mine was murdered in her apartment across the street from where I lived. I had just about enough loss by that point to last me a lifetime. I had absolutely no ability to cope with little stresses at the time, and tragically losing a close friend was more than enough of an excuse for me to give up. This is right around the time I found myself hospitalized four times in such a short period of time.

Can you imagine what the young lady I had just met must have been thinking of me? I can only imagine what her friends and family would think if they knew how empty the person was that their loved one was falling in love with. She did not care in the least. What she cared about was supporting me during a time in my life when I was incapable of loving myself. She saw something of tremendous value in me. What she saw was a soul that was redeemable. With her entire life ahead of her, with her natural beauty, confidence, and ambition to become anything she wanted to become in her life, she paused and saw a broken, bloody, weakened, lifeless person who still had much to offer this world, and she offered me friendship. She extended grace to me. She listened as I cried. She searched for my lifeless body at times in darkness. She did not give up, and she stuck by my side through every minute, hour, day, month, and year of my painful recovery back to life.

In this brief but true description of who I refer to as my angel many times when I speak of her, I now return to the previous topic of shunning. I can totally understand if people felt it was necessary to shun me as I had caused them pain. I can only imagine the anguish and sadness others felt when they heard I had made an attempt on my life, then another, another, and one more. I can only say that I was in such painful misery and was desiring to extinguish it. I have offered and still offer heartfelt remorse for stirring up these painful emotions in the hearts of loved ones, but what exactly did my beautiful dear friend and now partner do to deserve shunning? As the Lord hung from His cross, some of His last words were captured in Luke 23:34 when He said, "Father, forgive them, for they know not what they do."

If others had known of the heroism and true Christian faith expressed by my dear partner and friend, they would have carried her on their shoulders with such gratitude and love. She did *exactly* what Christ asked of her, barely knowing who He was. I saw Christ in her in those moments and knew it was Him when I found myself unable to repay the debt. Why was she shunned? For the same reason most Catholics shun anyone: she was not living up to the Christian code that they imagined in their minds. She was dating a formerly married man. Even worse, we began to live together after a few years. Maybe we were a package deal. Maybe most of the shunning was intended for me and she just happened to be in the wrong place at the wrong time. I honestly do not blame people for the treatment I received. I believe it was and even still is warranted at times. It can be useful as a tool for incentive to get on a path toward righteousness with our Heavenly Father. It all boils down, though, to one thing: relationships. As in the case with my beautiful and loving partner as well, relationships make all of the difference. I was once directly told by a fellow Christian that they would not come to my home unless it was for an event for one of my children as they did not want to condone my lifestyle choices. I could not help but think of the person I know who was in a homosexual relationship because "lifestyle choices" is an expression commonly used by Christians when describing the gay life. What I found most humorous about this person's comment was that they thought I cared for their opinion. I am well aware of what the church asks of me as a Christian. Different life circumstances brought on different life choices, which yielded the living situation I now found myself in. I was in no need of this person's opinion on the matter because this particular individual, among others, had little to no relationship with me to begin with. What was I losing by having someone who never came to visit me tell me that they are never coming to visit me? *When we shun without having the relationship to back it, we become the prize.* It is really the loss of ourselves that someone is missing out on. Often the offender in need of a good shun, as I was in this case, does not care, and years can go by without ever resolving the issue. As a matter of fact, most times, people are not going to be as direct as the one individual I described and the person being shunned does not even understand why they are being shunned. On the contrary, *when a relationship is healthy between two or more people and shunning is used as a healthy tool at the right time and for the right amount of time, it is likely God who is the prize.* We make it clear to the individual who is avoided for a period of time that *we cannot place our love for each other before our love for our God.* I feel certain that when we have accomplished the removal of an entire beam obstructing our own view, we will realize the greater ability we possess to ascertain the skills needed to operate the "shun machine." After all, if heaven is our destination, we need to help each other get there.

CHAPTER SIX

Heaven in Seven (Right Turns)

Just like a set of directions on a map, Christ through His holy church has gone ahead and charted the road to heaven. Even better news, we can get there by making seven right turns! No matter where our road to recovery begins, there are choices we have to make that get us to our goal. Every time we deviate from the plan, our chances of success diminish. The good news is that we can always continue to make healthy choices, and, with some honest, hard work, we will likely enjoy the exact results that match the effort we put in.

A perfect example of this is a lesson I learned the hard way recovering from surgery I had on my hand. Before sending me home, the surgeon told me to come back and see her in a week. When I was scheduling the appointment, I was told that I would have to come back in two weeks because the doctor was going away. When I came back to see her two weeks later, she unwrapped my wound and asked me to open my clenched hand. I proceeded to do so, but only my pointer finger worked. The three she operated on were frozen in the closed fist position. Immediately, the expression on her face changed from one that was relaxed to grimacing, and she asked me to open my whole hand again. It was the same request that yielded the same single-fingered result; only my pointer finger worked.

"Haven't you been moving your fingers!"

It was not a question; it was more like extreme disappointment.

"No," I responded. "It hurt too bad, so I kept them as still as possible."

My follow-up appointment with her was supposed to be in a week but ended up being in two, which meant that my hand healed in a closed position and stayed that way because the scar tissue bonded to other tissue, creating a tightening of my ligaments. She was very unhappy with me. How was I supposed to know what to do? All I knew was when I felt pain that I was supposed to rest it.

She sent me off to physical therapy. Little by little, the hard work of rehabilitation yielded tiny successes. I got tired and lazy toward the end and eventually settled for 70 percent recovery. It has been about twenty years since I chose to end the therapy, and every day that goes by, I wish I had completed the work that I set out to do.

I find this concept to be 100 percent true for my spiritual and mental health recovery as well. I will get the exact results that match my efforts. Getting back to the great news, my goal of getting to heaven is the most important one to me, and as I have been studying the words of Christ, I notice that He references Himself as "The Way." Likewise, He gives us a complete road map with stories and illustrations to help us along on our journey. What I have done is condensed the process into seven steps. Get ready for an adventure that will be filled with not only blood, sweat, and tears, but also happiness, personal growth, enlightenment, and guaranteed pleasant surprises. Expect to meet people that make you ask, "Why haven't I met you sooner in my life?" This rewarding expedition ultimately culminates in heaven, a place I have never been, but I trust that He who came from heaven knows the way back quite well. I have begun my trek and I am excited to meet up with you and others who desire to discover its summit. There is one last thing to bear in mind: no matter who chooses to join you or whether you make this voyage alone, open your heart to the discoveries that await you because what you choose to leave behind will pale in comparison to what and who you will gain. Your story is still being written, so do not be afraid to break the mold and get creative.

Now that we have properly prepared, let us take the first step.

HEAVEN QUEST
DESTINATION: HEAVEN (IN 7 RIGHT TURNS)
DISTANCE: Nearer than you may have thought.
TIME: Act now, but take as much time as you need.

MAKE AN IMMEDIATE U-TURN

First we must be pointed in the right direction. If we are going to do this right, it is imperative we face ourselves toward our goal. (You may not need to do this. I needed to turn my life around.)

RIGHT TURN NUMBER 1:

➤ MAKE A RIGHT TURN—TOWARD JESUS CHRIST AND HIS HOLY CHURCH.

Doing an about-face is the easy part. Taking the first right step is where things can begin to become challenging. If you are already a Christian, believing in Christ is easy because you have found Him already and have given Him complete reign over your heart, am I correct? I have personally confirmed my belief in the Lord and His holy church. I find that believing is the easy part for me. After years of studying the teachings of Christ, I have come to the resolute conviction that He is the absolute embodiment of God. What this means to me is if it were possible to pack God into a human body, the result would be Our Lord and Savior Jesus Christ. I am convinced beyond any doubt that not only is it possible, but this is perfectly and wholly probable, necessary, and true.

It may be imperative at this point for you to pause your journey and spend some time in this place. Heaven is worth the effort, and in Heaven, there will exist no trace of doubt. Every subsequent turn from here on out rides on our belief in Christ and His holy church. It is not enough to profess our faith in Christ. We must also confirm faith in His holy church in our hearts. To believe solely in Jesus and not in His church is to declare faith in a God that is the Head of no body.

St. Paul writes to us in his letter to the Ephesians, chapter five, verse twenty-seven: "That He might present it to Himself a glorious church, not having a spot or wrinkle, or any such thing; but that it should be holy and without blemish."

There are some things I have come to understand about Christ's church; it has characteristics that help us to identify it. For instance, it has the quality of visibility. We as followers of Christ make up His Holy body. Even if Christ's church had one member, that would still be enough to be considered His holy church. His church has three main identifying qualities: It is one, it is holy, and it is apostolic. These traits are how the Catholic Church describes the body of Christ, and it makes sense. It is one because Christ is undivided in every way. He never contradicts Himself; He is always completely in harmony with His Father and the Holy Spirit, and there can never be two heads to one God. He is holy in every sense. He is sinless and innocent of all guilt. He is just and merciful. No stain of sin can or will ever be found in Him. Therefore it is important that when we follow Him, we strive to be like Him. The last description of the three can become that of a stumbling block for those who do not profess their faith in Catholicism. Christ's church is apostolic. Today's church may look drastically different than it did two thousand years ago primarily as a result of how the pope, cardinals, bishops, and priests dress and how the beautiful basilicas and cathedrals in which they worship look. In the spirit of logic and reason alone, I would hope that if I were to exist for two thousand years on this earth, my investments in myself and my family would be noticeable, measurable, and abundant. I would also expect that no one judge my philanthropic works but God and that the fruits of my labor were plentiful and my family as numerous as the stars. So what exactly does apostolic mean? It means that Christ's church is inseverable. He has designed it so that His Church has a visible head that shall never be cut off. Our role as members of His body is to allow our faith to shine through our beings as a beacon of light to guide others toward the shore where they will find their rest in Christ's harbors. In Matthew 5:14, Christ tells His church: "You are the light of the world, a city seated on a mountain cannot be hid."

As followers and believers in Christ, we carry His light within us when we live and act in a fashion that He does. Most people do not walk through their day telling everyone around them what religion they practice, but as the old saying goes, "Actions speak louder than words." When we follow Christ's example of how to live, we will seldom need words. As in the clever quip from Saint Francis, "Preach often. Sometimes use words."

If we consider that heaven is reserved only for the holy and innocent, a lot of people will be excluded from ever entering. As a matter of fact, just about everyone beside Jesus and His mother would be excluded from partaking in the joys and rest that heaven offers. The moment we sin, which we all do as we are imperfect creatures, we are no longer fit for such a divine paradise. In fact, there is no perfect deed we can do on our own that matches the requirements needed to take up residency in God's holy kingdom. If you do not believe me or understand this concept, imagine that you are a perfectly healthy human being. Would you allow yourself to be injected with even one cancer cell? Cancer has a dynamic ability to metastasize. I understand the Lord to be the only portal into heaven, and now I begin to understand why His body bore so many visible wounds. His wounds will not heal until the last person enters salvation through them. His wounds are harbors where we can safely enter into Christ's true church and find sanctuary and redemption. If our Lord were not bloodied, it would be impossible for us to be cleansed by His blood. In the first book of Peter, chapter two, verse twenty-four, we see the passage: "Who his own self bore our sins in his body upon the tree: that we, being dead to sins, should live to justice: by whose stripes you were healed."

RIGHT TURN NUMBER 2:

MAKE A RIGHT TURN—AWAY FROM SIN.

There is absolutely no time to waste with this one. It is the second right turn we need to make, and, oddly enough, it is the one I waste the most time with. Once we have turned toward Christ, we can pay attention to his advice. As a creature of habit, I seldom understand the urgency of my doctor's advice. It is not that I do not believe him when he tells me to eat healthier and avoid carbohydrates, sodium, and sugars—I just cannot seem to break the habit of doing so. I try for a few days and then fall back into the previously carved-out groove of eating unhealthily. It takes time and patience to break our old destructive habits. If you have an addictive personality, the task of sculpting a new life for yourself seems nearly impossible. You have likely tried many times to overcome harmful behaviors that have begun to cause problems in your life. Whether they are bad habits or calamitous addictions, we always seem to know what we need to do. We just find it difficult to take the first few steps.

When I was a little boy, my godfather would occasionally come to visit. He would rigorously shake my hand and call me "spaghetti arms." When it comes to walking upright and away from sin and sinful situations, I think I develop "spaghetti legs." I want to choose what I know to be the right path, but my legs lose all muscle memory and become weak and wobbly. I find myself quite often doing what Lot's wife once did before turning to salt, looking back over my shoulder. People who know me must find humor in my spaghetti shuffle: "There he goes, trying to be Christian again." It is a lot easier to have worldly approval and walk with what appears to be pride in my step than it is to put it out there that I have noodles for legs again. Unfortunately, my gait is not upright, and my confidence is misplaced and empty when I choose the path of earthly validation. Perhaps part of the motivation for writing this book is to give myself a break from all of the mental diabetes I get from watching television with all of my spare time. With regard to choosing to turn away from sin, in Luke 9:62, Christ said, "No man putting his hand to the plough, and looking back, is fit for the kingdom of God."

To me, this passage is like saying, "No one who wants to win an Olympic gold medal gets in shape by picking up a cigarette." How many of us care to be an Olympian? What if Christ said, "Only gold medal Olympians get into heaven"? That is literally the equivalent of how good He is asking us to become. Now imagine the kick friends and family would get out of observing me out there on the track at the Olympics (I can barely run to the grocery store). I can hear it now over the loud speakers: "Security, a spectator has breached the field." I know that I mentioned twice now about getting validation and being mocked by family and friends. The healthier we are, the less we will care about how others view us. There is nothing wrong with wanting to get along with those closest to our lives. It is well within our nature to want to be a part of something bigger and to not feel like we are outside of the pack. It is the compromising of our morals that should concern us the most. Turning away from sin offers us the opportunity to call Christ our friend: "I will not now call you servants: for the servant knoweth not what his lord doth. But I have called you friends: because all things whatsoever I have heard of my Father, I have made known to you (John 15:15)."

I hope one day He will greet me at the gates of heaven, shake my hand, and say, "Come on in, spaghetti legs." *I would rather wobble through the gates of heaven than sprint through the gates of hell.*

RIGHT TURN NUMBER 3:

➥ MAKE A RIGHT TURN—TOWARD GOD'S COMMANDMENTS.

I sometimes wonder if the measure of our eternal happiness will correspond with the measure of our temporal obedience to God's commandments. As a father, if I give my children a rule to follow, most often it is for their own good and long-term happiness. The obvious rules relate to dangerous situations that children just cannot comprehend at a young age. Obedience will keep them safe and alive, which keeps not only them happy, but me as well.

Today, the word "commandment" is not used as much between parents and children. If I refer to a command I gave, it is usually to my dog, who I want to be obedient as well. The word "commandment" is overtly authoritative and, for lack of a better word, commanding. There is little room for misunderstanding and misinterpretation, and it certainly leaves little room for negotiation. When God gave us the Ten Commandments through Moses, by which Mosaic law was derived, in essence, He was giving us Ten Expectations. He wants a relationship with us, and He wants it to be a happy one. Every happy relationship is founded on expectations that are defined between two individuals. If we take the Ten Commandments and look at them as ten expectations between a husband and wife, they would look like this:

1) I am your husband/wife. I expect that you first consider me in all things you do, that your actions may reflect your love for me.
2) I expect that when you use my name in conversation, it will be held in high regard and not spoken ill of or with disrespect.
3) I expect that you make time for me in your busy life and remember our anniversary and important days on our calendar that show me you are invested in our relationship.
4) I expect that when my parents come for a visit that you are kind and loving toward them.
5) I expect that you will not kill me or anyone else, literally or by demeaning my character and destroying my spirit.
6) I expect that you will not cheat on me and you will remain faithful to this partnership.
7) I expect that you will not steal from me, including my trust for you and my self-esteem.
8) I expect that you will not lie to me and that your dealings with others are upright and full of integrity.
9) I expect that you only have eyes for me and desire no one else.
10) I expect you to be happy with what we have and not desire what others have.

As humans, we do not like being told what we can and cannot do. We even tend to do exactly what we are commanded not to. When we look at God's commandments through the lens of expectations, these commandments turn into rules that we make for ourselves if we want to remain happy in our relationship. We can now view our partner as a *person* who desires to be happy as well and therefore realize that our actions can cause harm and injury resulting in sadness and a broken heart. Every relationship starts out happy. It is when we fail to meet one of these expectations that sadness and injury creep in. The *person* who desires to be happy in this case is the person of God. He is ready to uphold His fidelity to us. Our infidelity is injurious to Him. He gave us ten expectations that are the recipe for "happiness soup." When we fail to command ourselves to follow the recipe, the soup becomes bitter and distasteful. We rightfully equate heaven with the word happiness. If we are pointed away from keeping God's commandments/expectations, we are pointed away from happiness. It is that simple.

RIGHT TURN NUMBER 4:

➤ MAKE A RIGHT TURN—TOWARD THE TRUE FAITH.

How happy do you want to be? If happiness were on a menu and we had a choice of how happy we desire to be, I would imagine most people would pick the entrée that comes with the most fixings, sides, and the extra dessert. We want to be happy. Happiness is another way of describing fulfillment, and in this life, the one who works the hardest finds the most fulfillment in their rest. Heaven is eternal rest. Therefore the one who works the hardest in this life will be most fulfilled in the next. Just like happiness on the menu, it costs the most, and those who work hard can afford to order up enough to treat those around them as well. It stands to reason that Christ labored the most to not only bring Himself happiness, but also to every man, woman, and child who desires to gather with Him and dine.

Where do we find happiness? In Psalms 143:15, it reads: "They have called the people happy, that hath these things: but happy is that people whose God is the Lord."

Happiness is not naturally occurring within us. We attain it by various means but from one source. It is an experience, not a feeling. We ascribe happiness as a feeling that we attach to our senses, like the scent of a flower or the touch of a loved one. We can experience degrees of happiness when our senses are aroused by an external stimulant. These moments are typically short-lived and require subsequent stimuli. When you first touch your foot to the warm sand on a beach, your brain sends a messenger to your toe that brings the message back to the brain at the speed of light with the message, "That feels good. I am experiencing happiness."

God, as the source of the true happiness experience, sends out messages to His body, the church. Our church leaders are His messengers. Think of Holy Scriptures as visible thoughts in God's brain. We do not dwell in the brain of God; we are blessed to be part of His body, and a purpose-driven life will reveal what body part we are. He has called certain people to be His messengers. These messengers are, in fact, "mind-dwellers" of the Lord. When He sends a messenger forth to communicate the spirit of happiness to you and me, who are part of His body, He expects the carrier to return back to Him for the next assignment.

Our pope and all of our Catholic religious messengers have a grave responsibility to the body of Christ. When the message of happiness is not being conveyed properly to Her members, lives are lost to misery, confusion, doubt, and darkness. Our shepherds need our prayers. When we pray for our leaders, we are in some way calling out to them from darkness as a light to guide them toward us with the message of happiness from our Heavenly Father. When we fail to pray for and call out to them, *we* actually *fail them* and deny ourselves the message of happiness of Christ's invitation to His feast.

Following with the example of an athlete at the top of his or her game, the training regimen they adhere to is a vital discipline that encompasses the cooperation of their entire body. One little broken toe or sprained muscle can sideline them from achieving ultimate success. When game time arrives, one person will experience great joy, and the others leave in total loss. When we practice the true faith, we are working toward the finish line. Our eyes should always be on "winning" in heaven. *When we arrive at the gates of heaven, we are arriving at the meet, not completing it.* We are going to be asked to showcase what all of the practicing of our faith has produced. If we arrive there incapable of manifesting our acquired talents, we may certainly experience a loss that brings on absolute sadness.

Heaven is not for spectators. Its joy is shared by partakers in all that it has to offer. Christ is trying to teach us that through His holy church. He wants His body to be fit for the heavenly meet. Stretch, then take Right Turn Number 5.

RIGHT TURN NUMBER 5:

MAKE A RIGHT TURN—TOWARD THE SACRAMENTS.

Several years ago, my parish launched a campaign called "Why Catholic?" If I recall correctly, it was initiated during the season of Lent and then again later in the year. We would get together in small groups at each other's homes and study and discuss the importance of living a Catholic life. We followed a particular format that consisted of reading, discussion, and prayer. In my group were my friends John and Michelle, the hosts, three other friends of theirs, and my mother and me. To me, the question "Why Catholic?" is a great one because we live in a time where religion is quite often relegated to the importance of a flavor. Coming from a large family, I can see the danger of this mindset. If my parents looked at each of us children as flavors, a clear favorite flavor would begin to reveal itself, and others would feel lost or neglected. Instead, when my mom or dad needed someone to help complete a task with them, they knew each of our skill sets and were able to make an intelligent decision as to who was the right person for the task. The same thing goes for choosing a religion; as children of God, we are taught that God desires us to worship Him in "spirit and in truth." Therefore, we are tasked to choose a religion that most matches this directive. There are many religions out there we can choose to belong to. I have found that when it comes to tools and resources, none compare to the Catholic Church. There are particular Catholic tools that come in a set of seven called the seven sacraments.

The seven sacraments, which are baptism, confession or reconciliation, holy Eucharist, confirmation, matrimony, holy orders, and extreme unction or last rights, play a vital role in the life of a human being. The reason these tools are so valuable to our existence is because scripture shows us that each of these sacraments were instituted by God Himself to aid us in our redemption. He wants to save us, and He wants us to use the tools He has provided us to help ourselves find redemption and secure our salvation offered to us by our Savior Jesus Christ.

I have personally done a lot of research and comparison on different religions and what each has to offer and the differences between them. I have personally come to the conclusion that Catholicism rises to a level that sets it apart from all others for various reasons. I urge you, whether you are Catholic or not, to consider the importance of your redemption and salvation and come to an earnest conclusion of your own.

As in the other areas of my life, when I needed to learn tools like coping skills, self-esteem building, boundary setting, and so forth, I deemed it important to learn them from people who not only had a healthy understanding of these skill sets and were successfully applying them in their own life, but who were also qualified in teaching them to me. This is where all of the mental health professionals are recognized for their hard work and dedication to helping people like me find value in myself and assist me in salvaging what life I have yet to live that I may actually enjoy it. In many ways, I owe a debt of gratitude, and I credit them all for successfully accomplishing this task in me.

This is my view of the Catholic Church and Her ability to not only confer the sacraments to me, but to also teach me the importance of each that I may live a grace-filled life. Grace is an interesting word. How do we know when we are receiving it, and what does it do? Here is how I explain it. Imagine you are sitting in a canoe and you want to get from point A to point B. The fact that you are sitting in a canoe is meaningless unless you are sitting in a channel or canal. That canal is the path that has been carved out before us by someone else. Sitting in a canoe that is properly placed in a canal is useless if the canal is dry. Grace is the water. When grace is flowing in our lives, we get movement. When I felt stagnant at times in my life, it was because my channel dried out. We receive the waters of grace through the proper reception and use of the sacraments. St. Augustine of Hippo explains sacraments as "an outward and visible sign of an inward invisible grace."

Another way I find useful in getting grace flowing in my life again is something farmers do and we all do when we are trying to get a good yield in our garden, and that is to pray for rain. Which brings us to our next right turn…

RIGHT TURN NUMBER 6:

➤ MAKE A RIGHT TURN—TOWARD A HEALTHY PRAYER LIFE.

If you went to my high school, you knew where the twin bridges were. They were one lane each and positioned fairly close to each other. Every time the bus driver crossed over them, it felt like a gamble. New Jersey is notorious for winding country roads that have little to no shoulder, blind turns, and lots of hills. The twin bridges enjoyed all of these thrills and more. On the blind turn that went up a steep hill toward the high school is a beautiful barn that you always have to assume is hiding a car, truck, or bus heading down the hill directly toward you. I am certain that many times a day God hears the simultaneous prayers of children and their bus driver as they cross over the twin bridges. I have often wondered why they were built with only one lane each, although it is pretty obvious that they slow the drivers down and give people the opportunity to be courteous as one passes over at a time. Nothing compares, though, to the sight of the forked river below after a deluge of rain. The power of the rolling, thrashing water is a sight to behold, and once again all of the prayers are sent up to heaven: "Dear God, please don't let today be the day the water sweeps away the twin bridges. At least let us all get over them first. Amen."

As a child, the sight of the water was a bit terrifying, but the older I became, it was a sight to behold. The water moved with authority, majesty, and natural force.

It was enjoyed only for moments at a time; as I have stated, the actually well-made bridges were situated on a narrow turn at the foot of a steep incline. It requires your attention on the road and typically, as in most bridges, is enjoyed more by the passengers in your vehicle. The high rapids would eventually dissipate, and there were even times during the year when the waters were barely notable brooks.

I believe that one of the biggest reasons our prayer life begins to suffer is quite similar to the effects of a river. God is always blessing us with immeasurable amounts of grace. As in other aspects of our lives, our perception and understanding are skewed, and we fail to acquire the benefits His grace offers us. I liken it to a pasta strainer. We have been poked with so many holes of negativity that we cannot properly grasp nor contain the water of grace we receive daily. We allow things like others' negative opinions of us, self-doubt, insecurity, ego, and many other unhealthy traits to pierce our souls, quickly drying us out.

When we stand at the bank of a river, we are only getting a snapshot of a moment in the life of the river. We are incapable of seeing where it started and where it is going. Praying is like throwing a rock in a river. We expect it to be turned from a jagged stone into a smooth river rock at the speed the river is moving. The reality is it takes time to work out the rough edges. We are the jagged rock in need of tumbling. A healthy prayer life consists of patience, persistence, and gratitude. Like the pasta strainer, we need to spend time filling in the holes in our sides with positive attributes like confidence, self-esteem, reliability, responsibility, and self-worth. We cannot stand on the banks of the river and expect to enjoy the effects of what spending time in the water of grace can do for our life.

It was not until I was able to change my perspective of grace that I began to see noticeable and measurable positive changes in my life. I realized a few things; everything I need to get through my day has been placed in a basket and is already on my doorstep before I awake, waiting for me to unpack it and use it to my health and success. *God has set everything in motion from the very beginning of time, and every good gift arrives in my life at the proper moment, and God is never late.* Like an Italian grandma, He wants us to "eat, eat, eat!" He has prepared more than enough food for us to enjoy, and as Christ said in John 6:12, "And when they were filled, He said to his disciples: Gather up the fragments that remain, lest they be lost."

Grace is never wasted. It will be gathered up and given to others most in need of it who have "prayed for the rain." As we begin to realize the edges of our once rough stone are becoming smooth, we can now take right turn number 7…

RIGHT TURN NUMBER 7:

MAKE A RIGHT TURN—TOWARD FORGIVENESS AND HEALING.

When I look backward toward particular times in my life (something I only try to do when it is beneficial, sentimental, or for the measurement of growth), I see a man who was in need of a lot of healing. Much of my life was marked with adversity, disappointment, and tragedy. These are at least the first three words that have easily overshadowed so many good moments that would have otherwise been thoroughly enjoyed. Pain has a way of ruling over all other thoughts, emotions, and experiences. When I was little, I went to the state fair and got sick from the food. The memory my brain stored was of getting sick and all of the excitement and joy previously felt from the rides, displays, and shows were locked in a closet while the memory of nausea had free reign of my mind.

Maybe it is instinctual to constantly remind ourselves of the pain and misery so we do not find ourselves making the same mistakes over and over. It is when pain turns to sadness that darkness becomes us. Sadness turns to ice. We become cold, lifeless, and brittle. Our ability to process events in a healthy manner is impacted, and we find ourselves storing our necessities in our mental attic. Garbage that should have been otherwise disposed of now has run of the house. As in the example quite often used of one burning their hand on a stove, the brain stores that pain as a life-preserving memory, like near brushes with death that teach us what people or places we need to avoid. There were so many of these painful experiences and lessons producing so much mental waste in my mind that I realized the hard way that *I spent more time trying not to die than I spent allowing myself to live.*

Healing and forgiveness are very interesting puzzle pieces to achieving the success we strive for when climbing out from the debris of brokenness. Understanding how and when to apply healing and forgiveness to situations can either prolong or delay our growth or advance ourselves to new heights, understanding, and personal success. *Sometimes we need to heal to forgive, and sometimes we need to forgive to heal.* I have often described my inability to forgive myself or others as that of a prison warden. I cannot forgive someone who has hurt me, so I lock them up in my mental prison. Perhaps a common misconception about forgiveness is that if I forgive you, then you have no debt to repay. The reality is the longer I imprison you in my mind, the longer I prolong my own healing. I believe that more often than not, *forgiveness and healing are needed between those who love each other the most and who appear to need it the least.*

Just like when we live our day-to-day lives, we produce waste. There is nothing traumatic about it. We realize it to be natural byproducts of our necessary living. It is only once in a great while that something extraordinary occurs, like a storm, that damages our home or property that requires a larger and thorough cleanup. It is those little moments we bottle up that, without proper mental housekeeping, we end up developing unhealthy dynamics that, over time, create a spiritual decay in our life. I find this to be especially true with regard to feeling marginalized by our church, family, or friends because of our current living situation. We begin to feel unwelcome, out of place, and unworthy of the same gifts that others are enjoying in what appears to be their happy relationship with God. We tend to be hard on ourselves when it comes to kindness and patience. Even though the journey is mapped out and seemingly cut-and-dried, it is not without its own challenges. The next hurdle to be considered may be one that is very relatable to those who feel broken.

CHAPTER SEVEN
Use Your Best Judgment

I can confidently declare that the only job harder than that of a judge is the job of not being a judge. As humans, we have a natural tendency to scrutinize the dealings of others and pass judgment based on the conclusions that we draw. When a judge sits on the bench, he rules. When he sits in his chambers, he considers. When he sits at home, he rests. This reminds me of when I was in grade school and my teacher would send me home with a test that required a parent's signature. After a few poor test grades and some old-school discipline, I would get the much needed signature. It did not take me long to figure out that the best time to approach my dad, "the judge," was when he was at rest. In this case, it was after he climbed into bed. I would give it five or ten minutes and then knock on the bedroom door and say, "Your honor, may I approach the bench?" He knew this was not going to be good, but it was his time to rest, not execute me. Although he found my antics to be a bit annoying for sure, he must have given me credit for thinking outside of the box. I am not sure that I got away with that more than a few times. Other efforts to get his signature would be made when he was in too good of a mood to be ruined by my poor grades. Perhaps family friends were over for a visit and there was music and laughter so "approaching the bench" would have to be brief and grouped with other interesting things like, "Hey, Dad, can you sign this here test? And oh yeah, Grandma called and wants you to call her back after the company leaves." Those of us who can relate to the concept of being a broken Christian have likely already resorted to the passage of the woman who was brought before Christ and was being accused of adultery:

> And the scribes and the Pharisees bring unto him a woman taken in adultery: and they set her in the midst, And said to him: Master, this woman was even now taken in adultery. Now Moses in the law commanded us to stone such a one. But what sayest thou? And this they said tempting him, that they might accuse him. But Jesus bowing himself down, wrote with his finger on the ground. When therefore they continued asking him, he lifted up himself, and said to them: He that is without sin among you, let him first cast a stone at her. And again stooping down, he wrote on the ground. But they hearing this, went out one by one, beginning at the eldest. And Jesus alone remained, and the woman standing in the midst. Then Jesus lifting up himself, said to her: Woman, where are they that accused thee? Hath no man condemned thee? Who said: No man, Lord. And Jesus said: Neither will I condemn thee. Go and sin no more (John 8:3–11).

Here we can see that Christ did not tell the sinister judges that they have wrongly passed judgment upon her as Mosaic law spoke clearly on the matter. What Christ pointed out with temperance and measure is that He is prepared to offer His divine mercy to those of us who are most in need of it. This sinful woman was thrown at His feet. She was about to meet a dreadful and miserable end. All of her choices leading up to that moment were no longer in play. What mattered now was "Can we play god better than God? Can we place ourselves above the Supreme Judge by forcing Him to conform to worldly standards that demand justice and are desperately void of mercy?"

We know nothing more about this woman leading up to this moment in her life. As humans, we have judged her by her worst moment, and the law has to approve of this ruling as it is never okay to commit adultery in any moment. What she meant to her mother and father were irrelevant. Who she may have cared for in their dying moments just prior to her falling from grace mattered not. What her children would do without their mother, if she had any children, was not even a consideration. How sorry and sad she was and scared to die was someone else's problem. What mattered the most was the need to execute correct judgment on this woman's soul and properly dispose of her life. This is the ugliness of human rigidity. We desire to be so right that it does not matter who we hurt in the process. *We will find what we seek.* What we apparently love to seek is fault in others. Are we supposed to think that this woman from scripture was publicly caught in the act? I have a feeling these tempters of Christ knew exactly which one of their friends was likely up to no good with some woman and knew exactly where to look. I cannot help but take notice that only one person is thrown at the feet of the Lord. *There is a vast difference between brittle rigidity and the firmness of unfaltering, resolute wisdom and truth.*

It is truly great and honorable to want to correct someone that you believe is in danger of grave harm. If the peril is imminent and a moment cannot be spared, we have a duty as human brothers and sisters to intervene in an effort to reduce the harm that we can perceive is about to befall a person's soul. I suggest that, if time allows, before passing judgment on someone, talk with them about their life. Ask them questions about how they have gotten to the place where they are today and how you can act as a support for them in their life. Then go to a nearby church or the quiet of your room, pray earnestly for them and what error you believe they are perpetrating, and ask the Lord to show you what He wants of you in this matter and to give you the humility, courage, and charitable disposition to confront your loved one at the appropriate time. Do this for thirty days straight at the same time each day. I am more than confident that your patience, persistence, and determination to be of honest and pure assistance to another human being who you believe to be in danger of losing their soul will pay off. If you are incapable or unwilling to go to these lengths to care for someone, then maybe your motives are impure and self-serving. Perhaps what you are seeking is fault in others that you may appear righteous.

There is a stark difference between someone who is ignorantly committing error and someone who understands they are imperfect and are struggling to make straight their paths. The ignorant person may be easily corrected with momentary charitable enlightenment. A person who feels stuck likely requires much more attention. Living a productive and fulfilling life can become very difficult to achieve when we feel stuck to our cross. "No one is perfect" is a statement of the obvious that we may use in an effort to comfort ourselves or each other. However, nothing makes a broken person feel worse than the idea that others are moving about freely and happily while we are strapped to our brokenness. The truth is there are no perfect actors on the stage we call life. Too often what we experience in our damaged state are others who pour vinegar on our wounds by pointing out our flaws and struggles with insensitivity and unkindness. Showing up at church may in fact be one of the hardest obstacles to overcome when we are in a state of spiritual fragmentation. We are willingly putting ourselves in the presence of what appears to be a holy congregation, all the while feeling that we do not fit in. We look about the room, knowing that others may be quite aware that we are sinners and living an imperfect life. It is the very room that will heal our soul, yet, somehow, we are feeling the most judged, criticized, and mocked. Our seat feels like it is three feet higher than the rest, giving everyone more of a reason to snicker. Whether we are the ones who are running ourselves out of the church or it is really the sneers of our peers, overcoming this noise is vital toward the growth we will need to repair and restore our lives to our God and His church. What we have plenty of are excuses and reasons to remain in a broken state. What we need are understanding, compassion, patience, encouragement, and support. We need time. What we do not need are ridicule, condescension, finger-pointing, scoffing, and arrogance. We do not need it from others, and we certainly should not participate in it ourselves. For those who are reading this book who do not feel broken but may want to understand what others are going through, there are some things you should consider.

There is a person in your circle of family and friends and certainly in your congregation who is experiencing some form of marginalization. They are feeling judged. Their life may appear out of control. They are clearly not following "The Way" in the same manner that you are with your life. They look and act differently than you. They make different choices than you do. Maybe they are divorced and remarried. Perhaps they are in a same-sex relationship. It may be that they are addicted to some substance or behavior, or their child is. They may avoid you out of fear of condemnation or reprisal. In the past they may have wronged you or someone you love and do not know how to make it up to you. There is one thing for certain—they want the exact same thing that you do: to know they are redeemable and worthy of forgiveness and salvation. They want a second chance. Feeling broken or not, we all know that seldom does anything ever go the way we wanted or have planned for them to go. In life it does not take much to break someone. The scenarios are as endless as the individuals experiencing them. Jesus came to restore our brokenness by allowing

His body to be broken and nailed to the cross. All the while His spirit and resolve remained intact, giving us all something substantial to press ourselves against in pursuit of restoration. There beside Him as He hung on the cross were two broken sinners who chose two very different and consequential paths.

What we need to consider is which person do we desire to resemble as in the passage of Luke 23:39?

And one of those robbers who were hanged, blasphemed him, saying: If thou be Christ, save thyself and us. But the other answering, rebuked him, saying: Neither dost thou fear God, seeing thou art condemned under the same condemnation? And we indeed justly, for we receive the due reward of our deeds; but this man hath done no evil.

One of the sinners got it right, the other got it wrong. In this actual moment of impending doom, the reformed sinner rebuked the other, whose soul was likely to encounter a just and painful eternity. Realizing his own wickedness and imperfection, he turned: "And he said to Jesus: Lord, remember me when thou shalt come into thy kingdom" (Luke 23:42).

This is every proper act a sinner needs to make in order to one day hear these words: "And Jesus said to him: Amen I say to thee, this day thou shalt be with me in paradise" (Luke 23:43).

When the "good thief" got the blessed news of salvation, his heart must have burst within his chest. To hear those words from Christ Himself likely overtook him with inextinguishable joy and put an immediate end to his sinful life that brought him to the Lord's side at that same moment. The good thief made all seven right turns in a moment:

1) He turned toward Christ and His holy body.
2) He turned away from sin.
3) He turned toward God's commandments, especially when he asked the other thief, "Do you not fear God?" He then declared Christ as "Lord."
4) He made a right turn toward the true faith when he made the act of faith, saying, "Remember me when thou shalt come into thy kingdom."
5) He rightfully turned toward the sacrament of confession when he admitted his sinful life put him on the cross.
6) He turned toward a healthy prayer life when he petitioned Christ to not leave him behind.
7) He turned toward forgiveness and healing and received it when Jesus offered him the sweet words of absolution.

Nothing more is offered about this story of judgment and condemnation, and nothing more do we need to understand about how to interact with other sinners. When we live our lives, we build our spiritual home here on Earth. We build it in plain view of all who pass by and interact with us day to day. When we sin and "fall short of the glory of God," as Saint Paul describes it, we make visible design errors to our invisible spiritual home. That is when all of the "project managers" take a break from building their own homes to come out and let us know that we are "doing it incorrectly." The truth is we are all amateur Christians who will spend our entire lives putting up crooked invisible walls. If our spiritual house was actually visible to our eyes and not just our souls, we would hope to see a house that looks like it was initially built while the builder wore a blindfold and had one hand tied behind their back at one end of the structure and clearly improving in quality and workmanship as time went on. In time we can expect that it will be obvious that the blindfold was eventually removed and not only was it crafted with two hands, but had obvious signs that there were other loving craftsmen lending their skills as well.

CHAPTER EIGHT
The Hardest Pill

"And if thy right eye scandalize thee, pluck it out and cast it from thee. For it is expedient for thee that one of thy members should perish, rather than that thy whole body be cast into hell" (Matthew 5:29).

It is a tough message to hear, and it is an even harder message to live up to. Jesus had a way of making the crowd look at Him with utter disgust and bewilderment. I have a feeling these words were the cause of many people walking away from Christ, some scratching their heads trying to understand it, others calling him crazy, and some just finding it easier to pretend they did not just hear words that would follow them for the rest of their lives like a loving, barking dog. I am person number three. There is one thing I definitely do not like. It is when people who do not know me, I do not know, I do not like, or who do not like me tell me what to do. Our Lord's words have a mysterious way, though, of transcending time. There are indeed some allegories that He used that were pertinent to the time period, but after some consideration, we can quickly begin to see how His teachings relate to our life, and we are left with a choice:

stay and listen or walk away. Eventually, we all need to "walk away" and begin the application part of our journey. Hearing Christ's words is sometimes difficult enough. Applying them…well, there is one word for that: "fuhgetaboutit." This is when that loving, barking dog that is constantly pursuing us lets out another reminder.

Jesus's words are like ear drops. When applied through that tiny hole that God gave me to hear with, *I go deaf for a minute.* "I'm sorry. I can't hear you, Lord. Did you say something?" *Our ears were not designed for hearing too much truth at one time.* Is it not interesting how our ears resemble a funnel? We use a funnel to slowly fill a reservoir, and we typically use one when it is something of value we are trying to store. Unlike eyelids for our eyes, our ears have no built-in muffs to filter out sounds that we otherwise would have been better off not hearing. When it comes to God's words, this is not the case.

In the passage from scripture above, the word "expedient" is another way of saying "better for you." The word "better" can be found written in scripture many times. It implies options, and with options comes choice. When Jesus tells us that it is *better for us* to enter heaven maimed or lame, He is in fact saying the choice is ours, but the better choice in this case requires pruning and plucking.

When we think of pruning, it is unlike hedge trimming. Pruning requires thought and is typically for the life and health of a plant or tree. Its intended outcome is for healthier and greater production of fruit. A common choice we are faced with as children is who we befriend. If our choice of who we befriend is wise, we will choose friends who lift us up and we them. If our ability to choose friends is faulty, desperate, or self-serving, we may find out later in life that we are faced with some tough choices. I have personally been happy to give advice to many people about the company of friends they keep. Especially when working with people who struggle with addiction or other mental health issues, oftentimes the person's choice of friends has played a part in the delay of their success. Therefore the obvious advice is to prune off the "friendships" that are really not friendships at all and cultivate the relationships in their lives that are valuable and worth saving. These words of advice are never easy to hear, neither by the individual who is struggling, nor by his or her friends who need to put the relationship on ice. For someone in recovery, this difficult choice is often the difference between life and death. So difficult is this choice that, more often than not, it cannot be made, resulting in a miserable existence or, all too often, overdoses and death.

Jesus is giving us the same advice. He is letting us know that our vices are leading us straight toward eternal misery. He is calling on us to do some serious self-reflection about what it is we are doing and where we are heading. I have previously stated how easy I find giving the good advice to others, but *when it comes to pruning myself, I suddenly become "Captain Meticulous."* I take my time looking over the same choice that needs to be made over and over: *I will stroke my beard like a philosopher; I will scratch my head like an inquisitor; I will sit and put my chin on my fist like The Thinker, and all the while I will remain choiceless like the procrastinator.* I develop a love affair with all of my flaws. I become like the crazy aunt whose goodbyes can go on for hours, kissing, hugging, and chatting about one last thing, then wash, rinse, and repeat.

I have tried all sorts of tricks for abandoning my bad habits. I will tell myself, "Okay, I'll just put the bad habit over here in the corner, and it'll be gone one day." Then I go to bed thinking about my bad habit all alone in the dark corner like a sad little flea-ridden puppy I gave a home to. I toss and turn. I think to myself, *I'm feeling thirsty. Let me just go downstairs and grab a glass of water.* I stroll down to the kitchen for a glass, fill it with water, and as I drink, I decide, *Since I'm down here let me just check on bad habit. He must be cold. Let me find him a blanket to cover him with.* I go back up to bed. I turn out the light and close my eyes and begin to think how uncomfortable bad habit must be downstairs on the floor in the corner. Maybe I should go and check on him. I get back out of bed and go back downstairs, and sure enough, bad habit is tossing and turning and restless. This time, I leave a light on for him. Perhaps he is scared and lonely. I head back up to bed, turn out the light, and pull the blanket over my head. Then I immediately throw the blanket off of me, leap off the bed, run downstairs, pick up my bad habit, and scream, "I've missed you! Come up to bed with me!" Within minutes, we both find ourselves scratching behind the ears. What I have just described is a classic example of an unhealthy codependent relationship that I have with my bad habits. We cycle through these breakups and makeups just about every other day.

Just like those faced with separating themselves from unhealthy people in order to get some positive momentum in their life, I personify my flaws when I see them as that little helpless puppy. Many people would find it easier to put a person out on the street on a cold night than they would a puppy. A person would tell us off and likely walk away, angry and indignant. A puppy will remain right outside that door whimpering and loving you. Whether we call it a bad habit, a flaw, a character defect, or a sin, the reality is we know what we need to do with it. For me, the first thing I need to do is stop personifying it, then stop loving it. Then I need to stop giving it a home in my life. As difficult as it may be to correct the minor defects in my life, I am still tasked with living a model Christian life, which means I need to identify and take on the bigger issues that I believe may be getting in the way of having a healthy relationship with my God.

Sometimes God chooses the least likely person to relay a message to us. He seems to seldom make it easy for us to realize we were just visited by an angel. *When we think of God delivering important messages, we imagine ourselves to be so blessed that the sky will open up, rays of sunlight will spotlight a circle around us, and everyone else will hear thunder while God personally speaks to us.* We also think that if this does not happen, then God has never spoken to us. We will likely go our entire lives without ever experiencing the former and may have actually experienced the latter many times. In some way, the message we need to hear sounds less desirable than the person we seem to hear it from. So what do we do? We dismiss them both: "There is no way God is going to use that hypocrite to convey His holy message to me." *In our minds, communication from the Lord will be on shining ruby tablets with steam still rising from the freshly etched letters, secured in a harness made of pure gold, strapped to the back of an eagle that lands on a pedestal that has just miraculously appeared before us.* Instead, we get hit in the side of the head by a paper airplane that has what appears to be hapless scribblings on it, and we annoyedly crumple it up and throw it away. We would like to believe that the unlikely supernatural scenario of tablets, gold, and an eagle would certainly convince us to change our lives, but the truth is the message has not changed. Jesus confirms this in Luke 16:31 when He says, "And he said to him: If they hear not Moses and the prophets, neither will they believe, if one rise again from the dead."

He is letting us know that even a miracle like someone coming back from the dead to warn us of the imperative changes we need to make will not be enough to change a person. Changes that we make come from within ourselves. Is the word of God not more powerful than the one who delivers it?

When we begin to amend the way we think, we can begin to have eyes that actually see. Sometimes we need to look before we can see. *Looking is seeking, and seeing is finding.* If we knew a message from God was inbound on the wings of an eagle or heading straight for the side of our head in the form of a paper airplane, we would still need to possess an openness to receive it. Who has been conveying God's message to you in your life? What is the message and how did you receive it? If you are anything like me, you have probably uttered the words "I know" many times. We do know. We know what we get wrong, we know what the right thing to do is, and we know how to do it. Knowing is not the problem. Application is the real challenge. *We need to cross over from "I know" to "I do."*

History, as it is said, repeats itself. As in the story of Noah, the flood is coming and with it comes certain death. Noah received a message, and when he shared it, he was mocked by just about everyone around him. The message was one of salvation from an impending storm that would bring utter devastation to the world. The instructions were simple: "build an ark." The task was arduous, and I am sure that Noah could not have imagined how important successfully completing his mission would be. He had a designated amount of time to save himself and his family from doom, and he painstakingly set out to heed the warning from God. It required taking the initiative of cutting down the first tree. This is what we need to do as well. We do not know what day the flood will come, but when it does, I want to at least have a tree to cling to that I have cut down and shaped for the building of my ark. I have a feeling that as hard as it is to prune areas of my life that impede my personal and spiritual growth, doing so will only be to my benefit. I am not called to build a giant ark that saves all mankind—Christ has already accomplished that. I do need to start making choices that point me in the direction of salvation, that if my time runs out or is cut short, I was found to be trying, with the word "earnestly" written on my heart.

Hearing and accepting the truth can certainly be a difficult pill to swallow. It is also helpful when we have someone to blame for our imperfect state. Our next step, though, will be a deeper dive into the waters of self-reflection.

CHAPTER NINE
Personal Responsibility

I have this theological theory that seldom is any human guilty of committing a mortal sin. For many people, the notion of sin, even use of the word "sin," is an antiquated idea. If any of these people are still reading this book, they have tolerated my references to this "antiquated" concept thus far. If they stopped reading already, then all who remain are those who still use and believe in the word "sin," those tolerant enough to allow me to make my case who do not use the term, and others who may be open to seeing where this book takes them. No matter what we have convinced ourselves of thus far in our life, when it comes to sinning, we can call it what we want, but we all fall short of the glory of God.

What happened in your life that led you down a path of brokenness? For me, it was years of child abuse. I lost all sense of self. The truth is I did not "lose" it; my sense of self was stolen from me. Abusers tend to steal from their prey every decent and pure thing their victim possesses. When a woman puts on her makeup, styles her hair, and chooses an outfit, she is creating a fingerprint of beauty that belongs solely to her. When a man chooses a certain haircut, styles himself in nice clothes, and exudes confidence, he as well is creating his own fingerprint of visual identity. Picture the most beautiful person you know. Now imagine a predator overtaking them and shaving their head and painting them from head to toe with primer. This is precisely what takes place.

What the abuser is setting out to do is to make sure you have no idea who you are. You ultimately lose your identity, and they assign you a new one. You become fatherless and motherless. You become a piece of property in the eyes of this individual, and the word "individual" is only ever used to describe them, not you. All of your once shining attributes have now become theirs. What you have left is everything that is wrong with you; these things *you* still own and you will be punished for. As a matter of fact, you not only own your faults, but you have now been found in possession of their faults as well. They hate seeing their faults in you and continue to find every reason to assault you in an attempt to exorcise their own demons. Recovering from such a frightful existence may seem impossible. I believe it is absolutely possible. Not only is it possible, it is essential and imperative that we do so. One thing I have come to terms with is the notion that I will never receive back from my abuser the things that were rightfully mine. I call it the "Attic Effect." I would describe the Attic Effect as a *dwelling on things that were unjustly taken from us and never returned*. These items are typically personal qualities like self-esteem, self-confidence, dignity, honor, etc. For one reason or another, we seek them back from those we feel are responsible for taking them. We cannot accept that we may never get the closure from the offender we feel we imperatively need.

Over the years, when he felt the need to punish me, my abuser would take things that I had just received for my birthday or from a loving family member like my parents, Grandma, or aunts and uncles, and he would put them in his attic. It was one of his go-to methods of crushing my spirit and ensuring conformity when he felt I was in need of some discipline. Seldom would I ever get my items back. As a matter of fact, I sometimes wonder if my stolen belongings are still in his attic to this day. From time to time, I think about what little treasures his attic is harboring, and I would love to go reclaim that which is rightfully mine. From this experience, I have learned to not get attached to material things. I have come to value more important things in life, and when I do receive a gift, it means more to me than the giver will ever know. Unlike tangible material belongings, the qualities and personal attributes that once identified me that were taken in my innocence are not forever gone. We can regain what we were once stripped of. It is a process, and it will take as long as it takes each person to find their unique identity again.

Having been down this treacherous road has given me an understanding and a compassion toward others that I would have quite possibly been unable to understand otherwise. The first two items attained by my new self were understanding and compassion. Who gave them to me? The same person who thought he was taking them from me. I now can also understand how others who have had similar experiences in their life may not ever want to hear the word "sin" again. I can understand how they may feel completely broken by their experiences, and I understand that others have played a vital role in the development process of their life. I have been faced with the question, "How can I bear the responsibility of my mistakes when I have experienced such horror?" It is this same question that has led me to the first line of this chapter. I could not negotiate the idea that victims of other victims are spiritually responsible for crimes against God or each other. The first thing I have come to redefine in my life is the word "victim." Is the word "victim" an explanation of who you are or I am, or the definition? I am only a victim if I mentally remain in a situation where I once was being victimized or if currently I am innocently being taken advantage of or exploited. A victim loses that status by becoming a perpetrator, and a victim also loses that status when they become victorious over their situation or assailant.

Here is where personal responsibility comes into play. *I am not responsible for what others have done to me, but I am responsible for what I choose to do to someone else or myself.* When I chose to end my life, it was not only to extinguish pain. It was a continuation of a culture of death and disregard for life that I learned growing up. I was perpetuating the exact abuse that I once loathed. Subconsciously, I may have felt that my abuser did not finish the job of murdering me, so I would show him by actually completing the violence myself. We all find ways of ending our own lives when we do things that harm our existence. It is called "self-sabotage." My choice was to end it all very fast. Others may choose a slow death.

When God pulled me from the depths of my despair, He set me back on solid ground and helped me to realize that my life was no longer about me. My new lease on life was once again a beautiful gift to me like it was at my birth. It was a new empty slate that I could use for anything that I wanted to. Unlike my infantile birth, all of the memories of my experiences were still there. As I have stated earlier, I have a new appreciation for gifts, and the gift of a second chance at life was never going to get taken from me and put in "the attic" again. Relationships have a new special meaning to me. Family and friends have played vital roles in my new life, and there would eventually be one particular friendship that has helped me understand Our Lord the Judge a lot better.

As a child, though, I found it extremely difficult to make friends. I was incapable of developing bonds with children my age because I felt empty and had nothing apparent to offer to someone else in exchange for their companionship. If I had no friends, then I had no friends to explain to my abuser. There were a couple of times when I did attempt to make friendships and I was punished for the temperament and flaws of my prospective friends. I remember always thinking of him as a criminal mastermind. He strategically made strikes and retreated afterward fast enough and long enough to avoid raising other's suspicions. He was always developing new ways of alienating people from me and even others from each other, all in an attempt to prolong his ill-fated and unrighteous power over others. Although he may have thought he was successful in his attempts to turn me against my own mother and father by always speaking ill of them, *my heart had a safe room unbeknownst to him where my love for my parents remained unharmed and intact.* With this premise, when I finally was freed from this life, I was ready to rekindle relationships with beloved family and eager to forge bonds with strangers who would soon become dear friends.

As I have stated, one friend in particular has helped me to reach a deeper understanding of my Lord Jesus, who will one day judge my soul. That friend's name was John. I could not believe I was actually calling him "John," because he was a judge who presided over the courts of several local towns. He was tall and robust, with white hair and a white beard. He was even a bit intimidating to speak with as he looked you right in the eyes when he spoke, and he was a "no-nonsense" kind of guy. One day early on after meeting him, he turned to me and said, "Call me John." I think John wanted a friend just as badly as I did. Even though there was at least thirty years between us, we bonded about a lot of things. He eventually called me his "adopted son." Are you beginning to see any similarities to Christ? Our friendship consisted of dining together at each other's homes, speaking with each other over the phone, and he even hired me to do some work for him. There was one particular time when I called him just to say hello. He answered and said, "Hi. Is everything okay?"

I said, "Yeah, I was just calling to say hello and see how you're doing." He responded with, "I am currently sitting on the bench hearing a court case. I'll call you later on when I'm done." He answered my call in the middle of his work as a judge. To me, it meant that his friendship with me was that important to him that he was willing to answer my call while he was actively presiding over someone's case. If I ever got into trouble with the law, he told me that he could not hear my case because he was my friend! John called me his friend! This was a fairly new concept to me, and it opened my eyes to something else.

What does that tell us about Christ? When that woman was thrown at His feet, she was indeed caught in the act of committing a crime against God's commandments, but upon meeting Christ, they must have become unlikely instant friends. He refused to hear her case and therefore sent her forth without condemnation. Will He do the same for me? The truth is when we go before Christ in our final moment of judgment, there is no other judge beside Him. Will He refuse to hear my case because we are friends?

As in the story of the adulterous woman, place yourself in the story. When the part comes where it says the men threw you down at the feet of the Lord for committing the crime of (fill in the blank with your struggle), will you long to hear the words of absolution from Christ? Will you attempt to go and sin no more in order to cultivate your friendship with the Judge?

The reality of this world, however, is that if we ever have to go before a judge, seldom will we ever be able to blame someone else for our actions. We can try all we want, but when it comes down to it, we must shoulder the responsibility of our choices. Whether we go before an earthly judge, place ourselves at the merciful feet of the Lord, or "stand trial" in the court of public opinion, we must account for our actions and our behaviors. Just as I have opened this chapter with, the question of whether or not we actually commit mortal sins has become somewhat irrelevant to me. All sin injures our relationship with God and opens us up to a condition of brokenness. Catholic theology teaches that in order for a sin to be considered "mortal," three things must be present: its nature must be grave, we must have full knowledge that it is sinful, and we must have offered the full consent of our will. My argument is that, most often, sinners are committing sinful acts habitually, out of weakness, addiction, and even lured or deceived into doing so. None of which, in my opinion, express "full consent of our will." I also have argued that if we understood fully the grave nature of a sin, we would be less inclined to commit it, arguing that we can never really understand the complete nature of a sin and its subsequent effects.

This does not diminish the grave nature of certain sins, which can and may certainly end up severing our relationship with God, who will one day discuss with us the eternal fate we have ultimately chosen. If we have a desire to correct sinful behavior, whether it is grave in nature, as in mortal sins, or less grave, as in venial sins, it may help to think about why we do the things we do and why certain things have happened to us.

CHAPTER TEN
¿Why Me?

What a great question! Or is it? What I am saying is, is it a question? To me, "why me" is more about perspective. The obvious and first thought I have when I think of these two words is *Why did this have to happen to me?* It is natural to personalize things that happen to us because we are the only ones who can experience our feelings and experiences. One of the major tasks of my journey, however, is to help myself change the negative perspectives I have of my life experiences and find ways to use them to help myself. What if "why me" is not a question at all? What if it is a statement, a response, or an explanation?

There have been many times in my life when I have witnessed others being injured. The worst are the stories that end in someone dying tragically or contracting a grave illness that caused immense suffering. How many times have I heard people say, "Be grateful for what you have. Others have it way worse than you"? Injury and death are scary propositions. No healthy person looks forward to them. Even Christ Himself became deeply encumbered by the knowledge of what fate He was destined to endure. Knowledge of impending pain or death can paralyze us with fear. Jesus lets us know that it is normal to experience this. In Luke 22:41–44 ,we see:

> And he was withdrawn away from them a stone's cast; and kneeling down, he prayed, Saying: Father, if thou wilt, remove this chalice from me: but yet not my will, but thine be done. And there appeared to him an angel from heaven, strengthening him. And being in an agony, he prayed the longer. And his sweat became as drops of blood, trickling down upon the ground.

Was Our Lord trembling with fear? This passage tells us that He asked His Father to find another way to accomplish this task if it were possible. If not, He accepts His Father's will. Fear is not weakness; it is a naturally occurring emotion that we must overcome. Christ showed us that we are not to become paralyzed by fear. We are to take action. His action was prayer. He even rose from His prayer and walked over to His friends and recruited their support with an admonishment in Luke 22:45–46: "And when he rose up from prayer, and was come to his disciples, he found them sleeping for sorrow. And he said to them: Why sleep you? arise, pray, lest you enter into temptation."

We are tempted into paralysis. Christ is telling us that it is harmful for our well-being to do nothing when faced with dangerous situations that cause fear. When we tremble, we begin to perspire. It is our body's way of cleansing itself of toxicity through our integumentary system. We draw life though from our blood, not our sweat. Was

Christ's very life endangered by the mere thought of what was to come? The scripture above told us that His sweat was actually coming out as blood. Did His body expel fear that had actually permeated His blood? He could have very well kept this story a secret and not revealed it to us. He chose to for a reason. Although His heart shook with fear and anxiety, "why me" was not a question that Christ asked; it was His response. When our Heavenly Father asked the question of who would answer the call to sacrifice themselves for the redemption of mankind, His Son, Jesus, answered, "Why, Me."

Which of us, if we could, would offer ourselves in place of a loved one who was in pain or who experienced injury? If someone you loved was innocently imprisoned, which of us would not wish we could trade places and accept the other's suffering? We have come to see ourselves as broken for a reason. We have received the exact injuries that we would receive again if this time we were shown our life by God and He asked, "Who will endure this cross for Me?" If our suffering were not capable of refining our souls, we should avoid it by the mere danger it would present to our eternal welfare. In 2 Corinthians 4:8–12, Saint Paul teaches us:

> In all things we suffer tribulation: but are not distressed. We are straitened: but are not destitute. We suffer persecution: but are not forsaken. We are cast down: but we perish not. Always bearing about in our body the mortification of Jesus, that the life also of Jesus may be made manifest in our bodies. For we who live are always delivered unto death for Jesus's

sake: that the life also of Jesus may be made manifest in our mortal flesh. So then death worketh in us: but life in you.

We can expect, as Saint Paul does, that if we choose to be a member of the body of Christ that we will be not only partakers in His joy one day, but also called to bear some of the sorrows and pain as He seeks the service of those who are willing to respond with "Why, me." We are Simon of Cyrene, the once stranger of Christ, who was called upon to help carry His holy cross of sorrows. Simon was not the one who was sentenced to death. As a matter of fact, scripture tells us that he was just passing by. He was resistant at first. Maybe crucifixions were common enough back then that he was not even remotely interested. Then he was commanded by the local authorities to assist in carrying the cross of this frightful-looking corpse of a man. He probably felt the pain of the whip as it was flung across Jesus's body unrelentingly. He was likely covered in the blood of Christ within moments of meeting Him. I imagine he asked the question very loudly: "WHY ME!?"

Our Lord has the strangest methods of making friends. One thing is for certain: if we fly to His side and help Him carry His cross by bearing the burden of our own sins and more so innocently bear the suffering hurled upon us by others, He will one day turn to us like He did to Simon and say, "Thank you, friend." In response to those beloved words, we should say, "No, thank *you*, friend." It is in friendship with Christ that our salvation is found. It is in friendship with Christ where we find our eternal abode. While we yet remain in His garden, we must expect to be pricked by thorns and blistered by friction. The hour has not yet arrived where we will be called in from our labors to rest. We have to remember that given the chance to do this all again, there is no one better suited to endure the life we have lived, thereby leaving us no choice but that which He has placed us in already. Not only have we experienced trials and tribulations, but every ray of warm sunlight, every rainbow our eyes have beheld, every robust laughter we have let out, every cleansing drop of rain, and every single embrace we have ever received was specifically for us who chose to answer the call with "why me." We are not called to be miserable wretches for our God. We are called to be beacons of light who lead lost sailors home. This is why we are told to not wear our sacrifices on our sleeves. This is why we are supposed to wash our faces and brush our hair when we are enduring heartache. Our cries are heard by God when it is He who we turn over our sorrows to. Only He can give us lasting comfort from our injuries. When we broadcast our sufferings to others, we have already received the attention needed for our wounds. Sharing in Christ's suffering can only happen in the intimacy of a relationship with Him and His body that are one. Otherwise, we are observers, not sharers. Many stood by observing the passion of Christ, while few actually shared in it.

Like an alcohol swab on a wound, Listerine rinse in our mouth, or capsaicin on a sore muscle, being restored to good health will sometimes require us to experience a little pain before we can heal or be cleansed. Watching someone else apply it to themselves fails to improve our situation. There are nurses and doctors who have been trained to care for our spiritual wounds. These are the ones who have been called by God to the sacrament of holy orders. In a world where there is more brokenness than ever, it does not make sense that we are experiencing a shortage of these "health care professionals." It is disheartening to see more and more facilities that were once great campuses for our faith and our faithful shut down and sold off. If we are going to properly answer the call of "who will be there to help my son carry His cross?" we will need all of the resources available to accomplish our response. We will need our church to grow, not shrink. Have we wandered so far that we are slowly unable to hear our Shepherd's voice any longer? There is still much work to do, and there is a big difference between being critical and thinking critically.

CHAPTER ELEVEN
That's the Spirit!

I t was time to make some decisions. I have no problem identifying areas in my life where I am lacking, and I can easily discern what I do not like in others, so what now? Are you as expert as I am when it comes to this? As a matter of fact, it is part of our Christian duty to inform ourselves of ways that we or others fall short of the glory of God so that we may avoid them at all costs, right? It absolutely is our Christian duty, but I look at it like this:

Do you remember the excitement of beginning high school? We were finally able to choose our classes! That was empowering and quite a thrill. For the first time in so many years, we had the ability to exercise the power of choice when it came to our education, and for me, this was a big deal because I was eager to bring my grades up and having this option was the first step. I was able to choose classes that were easy and were a sure thing for acing the school year. I was not going to choose classes that were beyond my interest and abilities. After all, it would not make sense to set myself up for failure. At the end of the day, when my report card was viewed by the "parole board" back home, they were looking for vowels, specifically A's. It was of little concern how I got them, but only that I did. It was now attainable. All I needed to do was lower my personal expectations and increase my results. It worked! For the first time, I was an honor roll student, the powers that be were proud of me, and I could once again blend in with the "academic scholars" at home who were likely doing the same thing!

This is what excelling at faultfinding is like. It is the easiest class, it has the most students, requires basic knowledge of morality, and you do not need to be an expert to enroll, but you will be one when the semester is over. Best of all, guaranteed A's! If you really want to shine in this course after you have learned to find fault in others, pick apart yourself. People who can identify their own errors are going places. They have the best chances of getting into Poison Ivy league schools. Wait, say that again? A little slower this time. No one brags about that. It sounded like you said "poison." Oh, I did say that. *If you dwell in negativity, you will excel in negativity.* The greatest thing about a Poison Ivy League education is it always leaves you itching for more. There are reasons why many products have fine print. It is because a lot of the time it tells us something we do not want to hear. This is not the case with the message I am conveying to you in this book. I want you to not only hear me, but I want you to also believe that this process is working in my life and very well may for you.

If choosing the easy classes and, in the case with life, choosing the easy path, has gotten you itching for something more, then where do we go from here? We have a decision to make, as we did back when we were young.

This time, there is no review board to hand a report card off to, there are no classmates to keep up with, and your life is depending on your investment. Best of all, there is no fine print, only fine individuals. When we think of the "best of the best" in our military, we think of navy SEALs. Their training is extreme and arduous. There is no room for laziness, selfishness, and ignorance. They require bravery, discipline, and education, among many, many other high standards of excellence before someone can bear the title of "SEAL." No one is allowed to call themselves a SEAL who is not. As a matter of fact, even the lower level of military requires such a level of excellence that it is unethical and even can be unlawful for one who is not truly military to claim military status. It is called "stolen valor." To be a navy SEAL, though, would certainly be quite a proud achievement. I can see myself on the sign-up line for an application and being sent home by the recruiting agent. He would take just one look at me and know that I was not actually willing to become a SEAL but just wanted the title. It is not enough to want to be something; we must make preparations and establish a disposition. I cannot say to the recruiting agent, "But I know all of the things a navy SEAL shouldn't do. I can be there to point out all of their flaws" (and get them killed).

This same concept is exactly what our faith and our Christian way of life is about. Forget about navy SEALs—think of any field or industry that you are in and identify who is at the top of their game in that industry. How did they get there and what will it take for you to get there if you so desire? These are the questions we need to be asking ourselves. This should matter to us because we are human beings, not because we are Christians. Our survival depends on education and discipline. I have spent plenty of time in my life "faking it until I make it" and making excuse after excuse. I have schemed and manipulated, plotted and lied. *I have hugged others while pickpocketing their sympathy for me.* That is not a bad Christian; it is the resume of a settler. No, not the settlers who were pioneers long ago, a settler who always settles for less. *The more settling we do, the less we will accomplish in life.* This is not what "less is more" is supposed to mean. "Less is more" is an expression of simplification. Settling for less only complicates our life. Why are we considered "broken Christians"? Either we or someone we know likely were "settlers" who did the limbo through life, holding the pole above their own head. That requires no skill. It is not even the limbo. I am not sure what that is. The limbo requires us to bend and balance.

What do you want? Are you reading this book because you are ready to pack up camp and move to higher ground? I want to challenge the reader, "broken" or not, to look at the name Christian as a title to be strived for. For now, you are simply a human being who is considering getting on the recruiting line for Christianity. You have the desire to become the best of the best. In Catholicism, we call them "saints." If that is your goal, go home. Come back when you have the disposition and conditioning to first be a foot soldier for Christ. What are you doing to wear the uniform of a Christian? How often do you take that uniform off during the day? For what reasons do you put it back on? *The Christian uniform is like a wedding ring.* When we remove our uniform to revert to being a "settler," we are dishonoring our spouse. Most people have seen us wear our "wedding band" and know we are spoken for. It would be better for us to have not worn the uniform at all than to dishonor our Lord with unscrupulous conduct. It is bad enough when we steal the valor of the title "Christian," but who are we fooling when we handwrite "SAINT" or, even worse, "MARTYR," on our lapel? We are not alone in this. Most people who put on the uniform of a Christian are doing the same exact things we are doing. It is almost to be expected. When we are wearing our "wedding band"— which should be always—we are not called to war. We are called to be peacemakers and peacekeepers. If the world hates us and is at war with us, our response should be the offering of our other cheek. *If we want to lay down our life for Christ, we should first lay down our death.* Lay down the act of dying, lay down the spirit of lies, lay down the murdering of spirits and abuse, lay down deceit and selfishness. *Jesus does not need us to die for Him. He needs us to die to sin for Him.* We will never rise from the dead until we can rise from the bed.

Christianity is not the "easy class." Much to many people's dismay, all will not be standing on the "graduation stage." Why is there an attitude that faith in Christ is of absolute importance but requires little to no work at all to receive the degree? Most people drop out but never take off the uniform. This is acceptable nowhere else in life. What makes us think it is okay when it comes to enrolling as Christians to declare our eternal inheritance? We want healing without a relationship with the priest whose hands are blessed to heal. We want to feed without the church where we come to graze. Disciples of Christ are students of Christ. We have daily assignments and homework. Our priests and bishops are our apostles; if their names were Peter, Paul, Mark, John, Matthew and Luke, we would be rushing to sit at their feet.

Again, I will ask, who do you know who is at the top of their game? If you are able, ask them how they did it. I have a feeling they are still doing it. The minute we stop doing what it takes to excel is the exact moment we begin to fall behind. This is true for science, medicine, and technology. We need to always be at the level of cutting edge. We should never settle for less than state of the art. If it is our goal to repair damage in our life, we must be prepared to utilize every resource available to our disposal. There are all kinds of avenues of help available to human beings. When it comes to Christianity, our church is the source Christ gave us for all healing and spiritual education. Are you struggling with reconciling your relationship with the Catholic Church?

The reason I specifically name the Catholic Church is because, first, I am a practicing Catholic, and second, because it seems that much of the world's spiritual influence is either due to Catholicism or aimed against it. There is a significance to this that makes it all the more interesting to me and may require a deeper reflection as to why. One thing is for sure: priests are on the front line of the Catholic faith and quite often play a vital role in procuring spirituality in an individual or destroying it.

CHAPTER TWELVE
Father Kioski

In today's world, it is impossible to be fully engaged with society without having used at some type of interface. This is just a fancy modern term typically, but not exclusively, used in electronics. An interface is a device designed to pair two otherwise incompatible modules to each other. Another form of interface we are very familiar with these days is what we refer to as a kiosk. We use them to withdraw or deposit our funds into our bank accounts, we use them for information gathering and directions at malls, and we even buy a pretzel or jewelry at one from time to time. As a matter of fact, they have been around for a long time, and today they are more popular than ever. What is the primary function of a kiosk? It is, in essence, a satellite or miniature broker or intermediary for a much larger institution. They offer us the convenience of access to an otherwise cumbersome task of information, services and goods. When we use the kiosk from our financial institution, otherwise known as an ATM (automatic teller machine), we are happy to not have to interact with the human teller behind the counter who stands directly between ourselves and our fortunes.

We are seeing kiosks pop up everywhere nowadays. The larger stores call them express lanes, where you can perform your own checkout if you do not desire to wait in line for an employee to help you.

Although some of these changes were quite honestly met with resistance early on, they are most certainly becoming a widely accepted and greatly utilized part of our modern world. Having faster access is becoming so important to us as a people that we are constantly developing new ways to make what was once a very stationary and inert world a now mobile and convenient one. The term kiosk dates back to the seventeenth century, but man's introduction to them occurred thousands of years prior. That is where we meet Father Kioski.

Did we ever stop to consider that our priests are actually kiosks? Often, there are arguments made as to the necessity and validity of the priesthood and our priests. One of the most common cases made is against confessing one's sins to a priest. Another argument against the need for priests is what makes them so special that anyone cannot perform the duties and tasks that they do? Maybe they are not personally any more special than you or I in the fact that we are all human beings, but the work and services they perform carries a tremendous amount of responsibility with it. Case in point: if the manager of our local hardware store is accused and convicted of a crime of moral turpitude, he will be replaced by a new administrator, but it will unlikely have an impact on whether or not you or I patronize the store anymore. The same goes for a school official, the manager of a nearby theater or grocery market. If a priest, on the other hand, is accused and subsequently convicted of such, it is a much different story. The community of faith will take a hard hit, and many individuals and families may lose their faith in God. In none of the above examples, be it the grocery store, hardware store, theater, or school, will the executive at the top be held responsible for the actions of one of their managers. In the passage from Mark 14:27, Jesus warns of this type of danger: "And Jesus saith to them: You will all be scandalized in regard this night; for it is written, I will strike the shepherd, and the sheep will be dispersed."

This tells me that there is something about priests that bears a special connection to God. If the priest has that much power to cause that much loss of faith in not only God's church, but in God himself, then people must actually be making a connection between God and this man. Maybe this is why we refer to our priests as "father." Maybe it is actually God that we are communicating with and addressing through this man who is His representative, or "kiosk." If we reverse engineer this scenario, we can actually prove this point. If God were the "end user" and used the priest as a kiosk to communicate and interact with us (the CEO of our lives), and it is we who cut off or fired the priest due to bad behavior, then God has lost His ability to communicate with us until we fill the void with a new kiosk or priest. With this reasoning, we need the priest to communicate with God and vice versa for God to communicate with us. This is His design and engineering for a system of interaction and communication that He has chosen to establish on this side of eternity so that we "end users" may have access to our "fortune."

Again, I will ask: where else in life do we argue with the CEO of an organization that their business plan is faulty, inadequate, or unacceptable? There are plenty of examples in scripture where people are told to go show themselves and that they would then receive their gift. For Saint Paul, he was told to go and show himself to a man named Ananias who would give him back his sight (Acts 9:1–19). Again, in Matthew 8:4, Jesus tells the man he had just healed to not tell anyone but rather to "go, show thyself to the priest." Christ, who was talking to Saint Paul during his conversion and in the example of the healed man as well, could have very easily given Saint Paul his vision back, and did he not need the priests' blessing to complete the miracle for the man, but He chose anyway to use these individuals as kiosks for His grace to flow.

Why then do we modern-day laypeople shy away from utilizing the very kiosks that Christ has put into our lives for our convenience and benefit? If something is inconvenient, that means it is likely more difficult or cumbersome. Convenience makes our lives that much easier, especially when we are in moments of hurry and hustle and bustle. Our Lord does not ask us to make pilgrimages to the highest mountaintop across the world to meet with Him. Asking this of us would be well within His prerogative, yet He still does not. He offers us an all too often denied convenience by establishing a church with its branches spread out across the entire globe. Likewise, we must call on our priests to really embrace the role of being a kiosk for our God that we may not be denied the graces and goods that come with membership to His holy body, the church. In reality, we as Christians have the ability and duty to act as God's kiosks as well. We may not have the same goods and services that priestly kiosks do, but we can certainly be informational and directional aids for others who are looking to find Christ by living a life that is filled with good example.

Just like in the example of a bank, the CEO, with whom we are ultimately trusting our finances, has presented us with low-level tellers and even lower-level automatic teller machines (ATMs). These offer the masses a much more convenient method of doing business with the CEO than it would be if everyone had to wait their turn for intimate one-on-one meetings for everyday needs like deposits and withdrawals. Interestingly enough, the ATM is no longer the lowest level kiosk, as technological advances have given us limited access to our banks via our mobile devices. I have never met a person who has ever argued with their bank that they "only do business with the CEO." In fact, the CEO is much like God in the sense that we never see them at work. This does not imply that we cannot directly pray to God or go directly to Him with our concerns, but which of us can say that He has ever responded to us with an answer that we could hear? He does not communicate that way with us. He does though offer us His wisdom, guidance, love, and forgiveness through the channels that He has established through His church. I have never met someone who has ever knocked on the door of the rectory demanding to speak to God either. We know He is there, but we also know that we are somewhat delusional if we think that this is how He responds to our demands. Along the same line of reasoning, all who call themselves Christians may understand that whether they believe they can go directly to God in their quest for graces and sacraments or not, they still utilize some sort of godly interface in their lives. Most Christians have what we refer to as a minister, a pastor, or a leader of a church. Especially in the case of getting married, I have never witnessed a Christian ceremony where some sort of interface was not used as a mediator between man and God who oversaw and blessed the vows and union. My thought as a Catholic is this: all ATMs can access my money most of the time at a small cost if it is not a kiosk that belongs to my bank. We can certainly receive graces from God through each other, but there is something authentic and special I find in the Catholic priesthood. Our Lord has created this office not only for our welfare, but also our convenience.

I understand that I have simplified and condensed a topic that has so many angles to it that has resulted in why we may feel broken today, or worse, maybe why our relationship with God's church seems broken. Unfortunately, we each have to work out these facets of our life on our own and in our own time. It is not as easily put into practice in reality as it appears on paper. Sadly, with all that we read, hear, and see, it is no wonder that this has not only been difficult for many, but in a few cases (a few too many), it is the very church in whom some once had faith that has now harmed them. This was not the intention nor desire for Christ's mission. We must still find a way to move forward.

CHAPTER THIRTEEN
Crown of Thorns

"**A**nd the soldiers platting a crown of thorns, put it upon his head; and they put on him a purple garment" (John 19:2).

On the head of our King was a crown. It was handmade, not with flowers or reeds like we often see upon the head of Caesar; this crown was fashioned with a purpose—to mock, injure, and humiliate the Lord. Just like His holy cross has direct spiritual connections to our life, so does His holy crown. With the cross, we bear the weight and severity of our sins, and we persevere through them. The crown, on the other hand, represents a slightly different meaning to me. Specifically speaking, the thorns are what have got me thinking. When I think of thorns, two things come to mind: roses and people. A thorny rose symbolizes the need to take the good with the bad in life. When a thorn represents a person, as in the phrase "a thorn in my side," I think of someone who causes me some sort of misery. Christ chose His thorns. The connection is not by chance. The thorns upon His head are thorns He chose, starting with Peter. Our Lord knew exactly how frustrating he would be to His mission of saving the world, but He went ahead and selected him anyway: "Who turning, said to Peter: Go behind me, Satan, thou art a scandal unto me: because thou savourest not the things that are of God, but the things that are of men." (Matthew 16:23).

These were choice and painful words for Peter to hear. Can you imagine how embarrassing it must have been to be scolded by Christ? Peter was a man named Simon who was previously obscure and unimportant. Being chosen by God to build and lead His church came with a tremendous amount of responsibility and power. He at times needed to be knocked down a peg. I have a hunch it happened more often than it was documented. Jesus wanted him to elevate his aspirations to those of His Father, not to the achievements of men. Simon, who by now had received the name Peter from Jesus, caved in to the pressure from accusers during Jesus's arrest. He would deny having a friendship, affiliation, and social and spiritual ties to his doomed Lord. Jesus, as God, had the fore-knowledge of this and still went ahead and chose him. Our Lord found it completely essential and vital to the life of His soon to be wounded body, the church, to place the first thorn upon His own head.

Just like thorns strung together by a vine, Peter would eventually be succeeded by Linus, and Linus by Anacletus, then Clement, and then Evaristus, and so on, to our current pope named Francis. These men, once obscure and otherwise ordinary people, would eventually be selected to be placed as thorns in the crown of Our Lord. Some of these thorns would even be personally responsible for piercing the flesh of Christ, drawing blood and misery.

These imperfect men, in all of whom I am sure one could have found fault, were destined to become part of the crown of Christ. Like Peter, some of these thorns have gone on to be giants for our faith and made saints, like Pope Saint Gregory the Great, Pope Saint Pius X, Pope Saint Boniface I and IV, and even in our time, Pope Saint John Paul II, among several others.

In my opinion, one of the hardest challenges Christians face is the desire to put on their own head the crown of Christ. What I am saying is some people find it hard to accept that these thorns that make up Christ's holy crown are indeed part of the kingship of Christ. It is easier for some people to pick and choose what Our Lord's crown looks like. When Jesus was forced to wear this shameful ornament of kingship, I am certain that some of these painful thorns broke off and were no longer considered part of the crown, but lost to the wayside. Most, though, likely remained and, whether we like it or not, are part of the crown that was placed on the head of Christ the King.

Why does all of this matter? It matters to me because as I have stated in chapter 1, I feel that our Catholic Church bears a tremendous amount of responsibility for the brokenness our world is enduring. It is my belief that our leaders have been and are continuing to fail us. Whether the crown (our church leadership/hierarchy) is crooked or has been completely knocked off the head of Our Lord, it needs to be made straight. Show me one picture of Christ wearing a crown with a chinstrap. There are none. My point being that *we are not guaranteed great leaders any more than we are guaranteed great followers of*

Christ. When a king wears a crown, we know he is the king. If he wants to blend in to the crowd, he will take it off. Even during times when one believes that the crown has been knocked off, the king is still king and the crown is still His crown.

We do not get to choose which crown the King wears. Everything that happened to Christ and by Christ was His choice. We do not need leaders of our church who desire that our God "blends in." We do not need leaders of our church who seek the approval of men and not the will of the Father. To them, Christ says, "Get behind me, Satan," as He did to Saint Peter, the first thorn. What we need are leaders who humbly bear the crown upon their head, and by the crown give glory to God, not to themselves. They can achieve this by humbly serving God's children and remembering what an honor it is to be so close to the head of our Lord.

I was sitting in church some time ago, and I turned to my children and whispered to them a thought that had just come through my mind: "If this church ever goes dark, know that we are living in what may be the darkest time in history." It was unimaginable, but I wanted them to just remember this thought throughout their lives. Well, it did not take long for my words to come true. Within three months from that day, churches all over the world went dark; the lights were off and the doors were locked. I was completely beside myself as I am sure multitudes of others were. How could this be? Satan has found a way to starve us of our spiritual food and drink. He sent a pandemic across the globe that would strike fear into the hearts of our leaders and each other, and, sure enough, our leaders caved like Saint Peter caved when he denied Christ. What darkness Peter must have felt, fearing for his own life. Our Lord knew what weakness His church would succumb to; He had a plan and He still does for achieving His Father's will of ultimate victory over the perils caused by Satan upon sinful men. What we need is patience and humility. We also need to respectfully let our voices be heard, like tiny newborn hatchlings who sit in a thorny nest crying out to their mother for food. We need to not only pray for our leaders who support not only the crown of our King, but even the one leader in particular who will go down as either a thorn that drew blood or one that went on to sainthood.

We as Christians, whether we see ourselves as broken or not, need to reconcile with our church, who we feel has, at times, even abandoned us. *Night has fallen upon the nest of the baby birds, and something or someone has caused our mother to flee the nest.* She will return to her crying babies. Our leaders will return to us. The darkness that has covered the earth will not remain. *There will be a new dawn, as there always is.* Christ is the new dawn, and when we draw close to Him, we can experience the serenity that comes with His gentle stillness. What we need in our church is a revival. *We need to see grounds being broken, not spirits.* We need to see churches being built and used as the focal point of the Christian family. We need to pray for an influx of vocations, where our young men and women can hear the voice of God calling them to devotion to Him by giving their life in service to the least of His. Televisions need to be turned off and recreation hall lights need to be turned on where families gather to engage in good Christian interaction. We can do this, and we can do it in the spirit of newness that captures the essence of the good that made up "the good ole days."

This is not dreaming. This is the happiness that comes from abiding in the Lord. Our priests are our hosts to the finest resort that Christ Himself has designed and built, and He has been long awaiting our arrival. We need to not only tip our hosts, but we should spend some time with them and they with us. If our priests are too busy managing the affairs of the business of running a church, it means there are not enough of them. A priest's primary business should be tending to his sheep. Shepherds do not sit behind desks; they walk in the pastures with their flock.

If we are going to experience a renewal within our church, we need to see a renewal within our own hearts and minds first. The same kindness that we must extend to ourselves we need to also extend to our Mother the Church. We need to learn how to fly (do God's will and keep His commandments), and we need our Mother to teach us how to. Our priests have been trained in matters of faith and morals. They go to school for years to learn how to care for the needs of God's children. If we truly want to fly, we should first seek the wisdom of our "flight instructor" priests. All we are experiencing when we watch movies and television are virtual adventures enjoyed by others. I suspect this is a ploy designed to make us sit still for hours in order to delay flight in our lives just a little longer.

What is grounding the flight in your life? We need to identify the anchors that keep us tethered to the ground and untie them so we can begin to soar. This is the reality that awaits us. We will no longer be "keeping up" with anyone, but rather leading the way for future eagles who long to soar toward the land of freedom. All of this can be achieved with healing and forgiveness, with gathering together rather than constantly finding ways to divide ourselves and each other. *If you or I are incapable of doing this right now, then maybe it is we who are the problem, not the church.* Just like any personal relationship between two individuals, we tend to believe it is the other's fault that we are angry, sad, or hurt. It may be, but we likely still played a part in the disintegration of our own joy.

Our Father desires for His children to come together in spirit and in truth. We are denying Him joy when we find new reasons to remain apart from His body the church. In essence, we are telling our Father that our joy is more important than His. We need to release this kind of "wisdom" as it is unwise and unhealthy to live in this place. If our victory is not by the same definition that Christ uses, then our victory will be short-lived and likely not a victory at all. Our victory should be considered complete when we finally are present to witness the gold medal being placed around the neck of our Savior, not our own. Our victory should be final when we can witness our Lord trading His crown of thorns for His eternal crown of glory and majesty encrusted in diamonds, rubies, emeralds, jasper, opals, and every glowing, precious stone fit for the King of Kings. Our victory should be realized when we are there to finally witness the blood being forever wiped from the face of the Lord, no longer needed to wash the robes of sinners.

This is where the broken Christian's path to redemption and salvation culminates. Our journey starts with self-realization and ends with self-denial and the understanding of sacrifice, especially the one made by the Lamb of God who laid down His life for His friends.

Following the analogy of the baby birds awaiting training from their mother on how to fly, not all babies are so fortunate. Some get knocked out of the nest or find themselves having a difficult time getting their wings to work. Some birds even experience a broken wing. Is anything sadder to see than a wounded bird whose wing is clearly broken? We have all likely experienced this in our lives and jump to the opportunity to care for a creature that is so unlike us. We are mesmerized by a bird's ability to fly and want nothing more than to salvage the life that an injured bird may have lost. Whether it is with our Mother the Church's help, or on our own, we need to keep trying to not only salvage what life we have left, but also immerse ourselves in it. There is a unique beauty to behold within each one of us. Now let us start turning some more lights on.

CHAPTER FOURTEEN
Design-a-Life

We have now dabbled a few times on the topic of how we define ourselves, and it is certainly worth taking the time to dedicate all of our attention to it for the moment. When is it okay to be defined by something or someone? Think of an evergreen tree—at what point does it become a Christmas tree? Some may say the moment we cut it down; others may say when we begin to decorate it. Have we ever stopped to think, *Why is this tree a Christmas tree?* What was once an otherwise obscure, ordinary tree took on a whole new persona the moment we chose it as our Christmas tree. The cutting and ending of its former life gave birth to a new life. It is now a spiritual tree with meaning and symbolism that showcases the reason for this new season in our lives, when we push the pause button on the hustle and bustle of everyday living and make an extra effort to give of ourselves to others. Gifts are distributed all throughout the Christmas season, from the smallest gift of a "Merry Christmas!" to a stranger to the overextending of ourselves financially to someone we love because money is no obstacle when we give from our hearts. Does this once ordinary tree mean all of that? I believe it is sup-posed to. When we have the next opportunity, we should take a closer, more thoughtful look at others' Christmas trees and what message they are conveying. Some offer a message of simplicity, while others may appear to be bursting with joy and fullness. *One thing is for sure: the tree is not defined by any one particular ornament.* From the star at the top, to the garland that encircles its branches, to each and every ornament that adorns its tips, no one decoration speaks for the whole tree.

This is the very principle that we need to understand about ourselves. We are no longer defined by any one moment in our life, whether it was our greatest mistake or even our greatest achievement. In the same manner that we find ourselves rebuilding our Christmas tree every year, we must strive for personal renewal in our life as well. Perhaps the best and worst parts of the Christmas season are the same exact thing: when it ends. It is the worst part of the season because it feels like we are so quickly discarding Christ and His spirit of life and giving, while it is also one of the best parts because we preserve its sanctity and mystique by not becoming overly exposed to its meaning, causing disinterest and disenchantment in our families and within ourselves. By the time it cir-cles back around, we are refreshed and once again ready for the rebirth and renewal of what Christmas means. Christmas is not simply a celebration of Jesus's birthday; it is the birth of redemption and salvation. Christmas gives birth to our new year, where we find ourselves once again able to let bygones be bygones and afford ourselves and others the gift of new beginnings.

Our new year is really Christmas, where we begin the process of designing the life that we long for. For weeks leading up to Christmas, we have begun the process of emptying and dropping off all of our "faux ornaments" from the previous year that do not belong to our tree. Like burrs that have clung to our clothes that need to be picked off and cast far from us, we need to purge ourselves of misconceptions, failures, and delusions and replace them with honesty, successes, and a firm purpose of amendment. When we think of the cartoon character Charlie Brown, he is a personification of the synonyms that describe him: marginalized, empty, dry, and sullen, and his Christmas tree, which has become a signature part of his character, reflects it all perfectly.

We are not Charlie Brown; he was drawn in an art studio by his creator to convey a message. You and I are not cartoon characters, nor exaggerated caricatures of someone else's perception of us. *We are living, breathing trees of life that bear outward décor that reflects an inner spirit.* Like our Christmas tree, we should showcase those ornamental attributes and qualities from previous days and times in our lives that we cherish about ourselves while handcrafting new features that exhibit all that we love about ourselves. Who are you? How many words can you gather together to describe yourself? Are you a basketball player? Are you friendly? Are you a mother? Are you self-employed?

As you sit there and write down everything that you can think of that describes you, break it down even further. Are you a good basketball player? Why do you love the game? Do you have a favorite professional team?

What about you who are a mother or a father, how many children do you have? Do any of them remind you of your younger self? What do you love about them? Are you like your mother or father? What about you as a friend? Write down what makes you a good friend. Are you loyal and caring? Do any of your friends enjoy some of the same things you do? When we begin to *describe* ourselves, we realize it is impossible to *define* ourselves in one word or thirty words. There is no elevator speech for who we are. Who would you trust to aptly define you? If it is an impossible task for ourselves to achieve, even the best of hearts that we love would find it even more difficult to accomplish this. Is it starting to sound silly that we have allowed ourselves to be defined by alcohol, drugs, gambling, eating, depression, anxiety, mental illness, our sexual appetite, what clothes we wear, who our father was, what our mother did, who we were in high school, how many jobs we have had, what street we live on, or what car we drive? These actually say nothing much about us at all. These are descriptions of things we have experienced or things we have done, not who we are. *Who we are is where we find our true riches or actual poverty.* Who we are is a journey to be discovered and understood.

Our God has attempted to reveal His deeply rich self to us through revelation and scripture. He is God, but that is what He is, not who He is. He takes us on the journey with Him so that we may know Him a little better and understand Him a little better throughout our lives. Every word in the dictionary is defined using at least ten other words! *Yet we, who are far greater than a word in a dictionary, will allow ourselves to be defined by one?* We are a culmination of myriads of moments of life experiences but will allow ourselves to be described by one moment? It would be ignorant to consider this to be a viable way of thinking. Does it matter if we are referring to a moment of greatness? You have now become the CEO of a large corporation. Is that who you are, or is it what you are? Are you still a father or mother? Do you still have a loving spouse who supports you? Do you still enjoy fishing? Do you have a special-needs child who still requires your every thought and consideration? Do you still have a favorite movie or restaurant? As we can see, even our accomplishments do not define us; they describe us—and barely do that.

What, then, does define us? Our story is a good beginning. How about instead of having that burning desire to etch in stone *a definition of who we are*, we write down with a pencil on paper *an expression of who we are.* Take your time with the details as well. To know you is to love you. Describe this to someone whose thoughts you value with a story about your life. Listen to their story. When we take the time for another or they for us, look at it like we are spending time helping each other decorate our Christmas tree that tells a story of life, rebirth, joy, and an inviting warmth. *A definition implies an unchanging description of someone or something.* We are far from unchanging as humans. Depending on how old we are, we may feel that we have several different periods in our lives that have passed where we barely know the person who we once were anymore. All we really have in life are moments that are experienced one at a time. We are always in our present moment, and who is there to share that fraction of our story with us at any given time is always changing. We should spend less time worrying about *definitions* and *explanations* and more time *expressing* ourselves through the ornaments we use to decorate our tree. What we are really thinking about right now is change. All that needs to be present for change to take place is even the slightest difference than the previous condition. There are three things we can use to make this happen.

CHAPTER FIFTEEN
Thought, Spark, and Mustard Seed

Here they are, the triplets of success! Thought, Spark and Mustard Seed. Each are the runts of their class but nonetheless harness the potentiality of unimaginable and exponential power. Once set in motion, there is no stopping what each of these indomitable forces can do to change the world. The mustard seed, a representation Christ used to describe the size of one's faith, can turn an ordinary man into superhuman being: "Jesus said to them: Because of your unbelief. For, amen I say to you, if you have faith as a grain of mustard seed, you shall say to this mountain, Remove from hence hither, and it shall remove; and nothing shall be impossible to you." (Matthew 17:19).

I have never met anyone who has been that dynamic in their faith, yet I have still met some amazing and faithful followers of Christ who have done incredible and inspiring things with their life. What Jesus is asking of us is to free ourselves from the restraints that we oftentimes place on ourselves that inhibit our growth. *Our misplaced fear becomes a trip hazard instead of a step.* We actually can and do benefit from fear in this life. A little bit of fear can give us a long life. Fear of breaking someone's heart can aid us in acting honorably toward our loved one. When we hear the term "fear of God," understandably it encompasses a notion that God can crush us or wipe us off the face of the earth or sentence us to an eternity in hell. What if fear of the Lord was a fear of breaking His heart? What if our fear was that we are not doing all we can for Him? We need to be realistic; we will never be able to give God enough of ourselves. There will always be more that we can and should do to show our gratitude for the redemption He offers us that leads to our salvation. *We can, however, give Him something He does not yet have: our saved soul.* Our Lord has shown us that everything He experienced, enjoyed, or endured was done so by choice. Now we are faced with this same notion. What choices are we going to make that aid us in the transition from being a once-broken Christian, incapable of setting our lives in motion, to a "broke-in" Christian who is well-oiled, pliable, and adaptable?

We have had what I would call emotional and spiritual rigor mortis. We are not yet dead, but our souls have been experiencing the cold stiffness that, until our soul is broken and flexed, it feels unusable and incapable. The brokenness, as I touched on in my introduction, is no longer a negative view of myself, but rather an expression of potential. My brokenness is a readiness, like that of a baseball glove that no longer drops the ball, a new pair of jeans that flexes to the contour of a body, or expensive shoes that were once uncomfortable and blistering but now useful and satisfying. We are like the glowstick that, once it is broken and bent, gives off a unique light to be enjoyed by ourselves and others. As broken Christians, we are like the forest whose silence was broken by the chirping of the first bird at dawn or the dawn that broke the darkness enough to get us back on our journey. *We are like the glass surface of a pond that has been broken by the belly flop of a frog named Happiness, setting in motion ripples from shore to shore.* We are the once bucking stallion or mare that no one would dare draw near to, whose wild and aggressive nature has finally been broken and is now ready to be someone's friend, starting with ourselves. *Most of our relationships will reflect the one we have with ourselves.* If you take a look around you and you see several warm, loving, and dynamic people whom you love and long to get along with, know that this is actually the ripple of "Happiness the Frog" that leapt somewhere inside of you. It is not until we can get out of our own way that we will begin to see that maybe others are not so far from us who may benefit from the experiences and tools we have collected on our journey. When I felt like I was finally crushed by my cross, I was ready to resurrect my once dead self and pursue a path to redemption and salvation. I rose up and washed that "muddy mask" from my face. *I knew that if I was going to do this, I needed to stop hiding behind the dirt left by others and redeem my beautiful life that our God chose to personally give to me.*

Christianity is more than just a belief for a select number of people. It is a product. Christ has founded this franchise and rightfully expects quality. Whether we deliver this way of life locally or across the globe, it should be practiced with joy, honesty, and charity.

When asked what the greatest commandment is, Christ answered that we should love God with our whole hearts and our whole minds and love our neighbor as ourself. *Our self-love is what we use to love our neighbor.* This is the unmistakable sign of a Christian. We are a brand. Some of the best branded products require no words at all to identify them. If you look at a pair of Jordan sneakers, you know by their very design and quality what they are. The iPhone, the SOLO cup, the Fig Newton, the Q-Tip, Post-it Notes, and the Sharpie marker are all examples of product brands that are easily identified by sight. This is the same concept we as Christians should be conveying. The authentic ingredients Christ chose to identify a Christian are love (for His Father, our God, ourselves, and each other), patience, kindness, joy, mercy and forgiveness, humility, selflessness, flexibility, honesty, and every good and kind characteristic. *These all originate in Him and should culminate within us.*

How many of our thoughts fade like vapor? Write your thoughts down, record them, verbalize them to someone you respect. Even if it turns out that your thought is irrational, unrealistic, or unattainable, it may cause you to answer it with a thoughtful response that deserves a second consideration. It takes one thought to bring about change. *It is disheartening to think that there have been more sparks that have lit cigarettes than have been used to light the world on fire with change.* We need to change that, and we can change that. Action first requires a thought, and a fire first requires a spark. We are no longer controlled by lies, misconceptions, delusions, and irrationality. We have taken back the role of defining who we are and the name by which others are to call us. *We are no longer defined by words but use words to define ourselves, not confine ourselves.* Words should no longer have power over us; rather, they are tools to convey to others our message of life. *Our eyes should be the balcony that others can see heaven from.* Our open hearts should be as a soft pillow for Christ's head. When we embrace truth, whether it be about ourselves, another person, or our God, we embrace life. *There will be no strangers in paradise and no friends in hell.*

Who has brought the love of Christ to your life? Was it your beloved grandma? Was it your child who looks at you with what you believe to be undeserved admiration? He or she said, "I love you," because they really do. Was it your neighbor who cared for you when you needed a hand? Was it the cashier at the grocery store whose smile and quiet service was deeply appreciated? Who has showed you what unconditional love is like? Who has carried Christ's lantern to light the darkness before you? Was it your doctor who forgave a bill? How about your mail carrier who seldom gets a thank you? Was it the young mother who is working an extra job hosting at a restaurant? She greeted you with kind welcome and sat you in your favorite seat, but her heart was broken because her baby's father does not want to be a part of her life anymore, but you never knew that because her job is to make you happy. Is it your spouse who feels safe in your company, who knows everything about you and wants you to feel safe in theirs? Was it your high school teacher or coach who understood how valuable your future is and shared their wisdom with you and whose only desire was to see you succeed? Was it a devoted friend who was always there to brighten your day or walk you through your grief? *We all know someone who our Lord has placed in our life who has added "friend of Christ" to their spiritual resume.* I was moved once by the sight of a flower that grew in the crack of a busy sidewalk. It defied all of the odds of getting trampled, or perhaps others were moved by it as well. It was during the darkest time in my life and gave me inspiration to live and take chances worth taking. Even our pets that spring up to meet us the moment we walk through the door have an ability to ignite something that shines within us. These are all the spark that Jesus keeps striking to ignite a purge within us. Will you send them away defeated and unsuccessful? Who will we carry the light of Christ to? Do you know anyone right now who is having a thought about changing their life for the better? Fly to their side and see if you can help them turn that thought into an action. Listen to them and try to understand what resources they possess that they can use to advance their situation. Your tiny acts of faith and friendship will be cultivated in time and season to the glory of God. Your faith will be rewarded as you are serving your Lord as His tiny mustard seed; a seed that is unrecognizable as it has compounded in growth into the wonderful fortress of a mustard tree. This is not what awaits us; this is the victory that becomes us. *We easily become defeated because the Polaroid has not yet developed.* It takes time to see the whole picture and even more to see it clearly. It will take however long it needs to take. Be patient. What happens next is…

9 781638 372486